*"I commend to
you our sister Phoebe,
a deacon of the church in
Cenchreae. I ask you to receive
her in the Lord in a way worthy of
his people and to give her any help she
may need from you, for she has been
the benefactor of many people,
including me."*

—ROMANS 16:1–2 (NIV)

Ordinary Women of the BIBLE

✦

Ordinary Women of the BIBLE

A PERILOUS JOURNEY
PHOEBE'S STORY

MARY DeMUTH

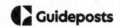

Cover and interior design by Müllerhaus

Cover illustration by Brian Call and nonfiction illustrations by Nathalie Beauvois, both represented by Online Illustration LLC.

Typeset by Aptara, Inc.

ISBN 978-1-961126-50-3 (hardcover)
ISBN 978-1-951015-36-7 (epub)

Printed and bound in the United States of America

10 9 8 7 6 5 4 3 2 1

Ordinary Women of the BIBLE

❖

A PERILOUS JOURNEY
PHOEBE'S STORY

To Dr. Sandra Glahn, who has pioneered
a theological way through.

ACKNOWLEDGMENTS

I am grateful for the scholarship behind the life of Phoebe, without which I could not have explored her possible journey. I simply stand on the shoulders of historians and biblical scholars, which is a humbling position.

Gratitude abounds for the Writing Prayer Circle, who have prayed for me for more than fifteen years now—all faithful friends. Thank you, Kathi, Sandi, Holly, Renee, Caroline, Cheramy, Jeanne, D'Ann, Darren, Dorian, Erin, Helen, Katy G., Katy R., Anita, Diane, Cyndi, Leslie, Liz, Rebecca, Sarah, Tim, Tina, Nicole, Tosca, TJ, Patrick, Jody, Susan, Becky, Dena, Carol, Susie, Christy, Alice, Randy, Paul, Jan, Thomas, Judy, Aldyth, Sue, Brandilyn, Lisa, Richard, Michele, Yanci, Cristin, Roy, Michelle, Ocieanna, Denise, Heidi, Kristin, Sarah, Phyllis, Emilie, Lea Ann, Boz, Patricia, Anna, Kendra, Gina, Ralph, Sophie, Anna, Jodie, Hope, Ellen, Lacy, Tracy, Susie May, Becky, Paula, John, Julie, Dusty, Tabea, Jessica, Cheri, Shelley, Elain, Ally, Lilly, Sabina, and Amy. As I've written before: any success in terms of the kingdom comes in the joyful aftermath of your prayers.

Gratitude for David Van Diest, an even-tempered agent who has undergirded my career. And thank you to Guideposts for believing in and shepherding this project. I am indebted to you and so very grateful for your editorial prowess.

Huge thanks to my family—husband Patrick and three amazing adult children, Sophie, Aidan, and Julia—who welcome my storytelling and always tell the best stories.

Jesus, You are my all, my reason, my hope. May I be as captured by You as Phoebe was, and may I always see our relationship as an adventure. The glory? It goes to You.

Glossary of
TERMS

aureus • basic gold unit in Roman Empire worth 25 silver **denarii;** a denarii equals 10 bronze asses

asses • one-tenth of a danarius

domus • the name for a modest home

fibulae • a clasp or a brooch

impluvium • a part of a house open to the sky with a pool beneath it to catch rainwater

oikos • a house or dwelling, a spiritual house or structure, a household or family, a possible term for a fellowship of believers

palla • a long shawl used to wrap shoulders and head

peristyle • a courtyard area at the back of a typical house during this era

stola • a long dress-like garment worn over a tunic, some wool, some silk, or linen for the wealthy

stadia • much less than a mile, equal to 125 **passus** (similar to a man's pace)

CHAPTER ONE

Cenchreae, AD 58

I cannot." Phoebe sat on a stone bench in her villa's atrium, smoothing her linen *stola* in a vain effort to keep her hands from trembling. For a brief moment, she allowed her gaze to look up at Paul. His piercing scrutiny weakened her resolve to stand firm in her refusal to his request. She bowed her head once more.

"I cannot," she repeated. In the periphery of her vision, she saw the intense man begin to pace. Then he paused and sat on a bench opposite her. His very presence demanded she look at him.

"You're the one I trust, Phoebe." His tone softened when he spoke her name. "And you're the one with means. You're our Esther, raised up for a time such as this."

His earnestness stole her voice in that moment. The weight of his words burdened her heart. True, God had rescued her... and ruined her. And yet, though He slay her, she would remain wholly committed to the cause of Christ.

Paul, the apostle to the Gentiles, the earnest disciple of Yeshua, stood again. "You remember my words, don't you? About fools?"

She nodded and reached for an earthen cup, slaking her dried throat with clear water. "Yes, yes, of course."

"God doesn't call the clever. He doesn't chase the wise. He looks for the weak. He uses those the world considers foolish to shame the learned. These are the people who bring Him glory, the ones who allow His reputation to shine—to shine like your name, Woman of Light."

He spoke the truth. Her name, Phoebe, meant "light." However, until she met Yeshua, her life had been shrouded in a gray fog. She had never quite been able to see things clearly. She chased after success and a high reputation for herself, for her husband, for their endeavors. But even as good fortune upon good fortune graced their household, her heart shrank with each victory. The fog gave way to darkness, and she was left hoping there was more to life than what she'd found. She swallowed the memories that threatened to strangle her. "I am no one, Paul," she said, shaking her head. "There must be someone better equipped to do what you are asking."

Paul paced before the *impluvium* as the sun danced upon the captured rainwater. "Regardless of what you think, I am convinced you are the one the Almighty has called to do this task."

"You forget my gender," Phoebe said.

"There is neither male nor female, Jew nor Greek...." Paul's voice trailed.

"But a widow? Alone in the world? Shunned by all? Who am I that you would ask such a request?" She studied the gold rings on her fingers. "There are some things not even my wealth can buy."

"You call yourself shunned," Paul replied. "And that is true. You have been forsaken by everyone—by father and mother, aunt and uncle, by in-laws and neighbors, by death itself as it ceased your husband's breath. What you say is wholly accurate." Paul paused just long enough to let his words sink in; but when he spoke again, his voice was barely above a whisper. "Have you forgotten the great reversal of the kingdom of God, Phoebe? That you are dearly loved? A child of the God who created it all? You are a deacon in His church, a wise steward of wealth, a chosen person, a minister of Yeshua, the Christ. You have been bought with a price. And now I ask you to spend yourself for Him."

She sighed then stood to match his gaze. "When you say it that way..."

"I'm not trying to woo you with clever words, Phoebe. I simply ask you to pray and seek His will in the matter, as I have. I'd certainly go myself if I could. This scroll contains my heart, the very words of the Lord for a people in desperate need in Rome. Priscilla and Aquila need these words. The *oikos* needs them. Would you carry them for me? Please?"

Phoebe watched the sun dip beneath the roofline of her inner courtyard. She shivered. "I will pray. This is a decision that must not be made without careful consideration."

Paul inclined his head. "Yes, this involves far more than a journey."

She walked beside him toward the outer portico, where roses had escaped their confines and scrambled up the stone walls, scenting their way.

Now in the street, Paul's eyes moistened. "There will no doubt be danger. I cannot promise otherwise."

"That is not the reason for my reticence," Phoebe said.

"What is it, then?" Paul beckoned her to follow him on the path. The sun fairly danced upon the early evening, casting the world in vibrant light and depth of shadow. They walked in silence while the sun dipped lower on the horizon and the shadows grew like trees behind them.

How could she express what was in her heart? This request weighted itself with expectation, and she feared she would dash Paul's hopes. She remembered his letter when he called her body of believers to account, when Marcus slept with his father's wife without shame. Paul had shed holy light not simply upon the fornication but laid blame at the feet of the entire church for not bringing this transgression to the forefront. She had been afraid to call out such darkness herself, reasoning they could move forward, forgetting Marcus's sin, and continue serving their Savior. But Paul spoke of leaven—that even a little yeast of sin permeates the entire dough—and soon Marcus's sin would knead its way through their body of believers. Paul wanted them to be what he called "unleavened bread of sincerity and truth." They were to deliver Marcus to Satan, the adversary, in hopes that he would turn from his incestuous ways. Expelling him meant they would welcome the holiness of God back into their midst. And so they did.

And, miraculously, when they chastised Marcus, he eventually repented, while Paul encouraged them all to welcome him back as a brother—with loving-kindness.

"I may fail you," Phoebe finally managed.

"I am not God. I am not the one to hold you accountable. I am simply asking you to consider my request."

The early evening quieted while birds sang lazy songs, and the air thickened with surprising humidity.

"It is a long journey for a woman alone," she said into the cooling air. "I trust only Trecia to accompany me, but two women traveling alone will be an anomaly in the empire."

Paul laughed then, a full-hearted, rare explosion that seemed to erupt from his lungs. "I would not ask you to make such a journey without a guard, Phoebe. Joses will go with you. He is trustworthy, strong, and capable."

"I do not know him." Fear gripped her heart. However, not in the way one might think. No, she had been a married woman, acquainted with the ways of men. But even now, her father's contorted face still haunted her, his words of wrath and rancor piercing her heart with the same fresh pain as it had then.

When Phoebe had proclaimed the name of Jesus as Lord, her mother's pleas had injured Phoebe's heart. Yet it was her father's unconditional abandonment that strangled her. Her parents' love swiftly terminated at the mention of His name. Even so, she could not, would not, betray Yeshua. If she thought she knew her father and he turned his back, what betrayal might a stranger be capable of? Still, she trusted Paul, believed his words. Surely this man he recommended represented his same integrity.

"He will protect you. You must allow him to accompany you." Paul's words wove between them, stringing an air of authority, tinted with fatherly concern.

Phoebe turned. "It will be getting dark soon. I need to get back inside. But let me assure you, I will pray about this endeavor."

Paul returned her to her villa, nodded again in the fading light. "I cannot overemphasize the importance of this request, Phoebe. These words need to find their way into the hearts and minds of the Roman believers. God has shown me as much. And I believe you are the person to bring this about."

She lingered beneath the tangle of roses then sighed as the apostle to the Gentiles ambled back down the path. His eyes strained, she knew, at the darkness. To navigate, he traced his fingers along the stone wall to his right.

"My lady?" Trecia startled her from behind.

Phoebe tried to shed the weight of the conversation, tried to appear lighthearted, carefree. "Yes, Trecia?"

"I have prepared some roasted lamb and dates, and a little cheese. It is time for your evening meal." Trecia motioned Phoebe inside, where her supper had been spread out on a low table.

Phoebe ate in silence, wrangling Paul's words, chewing on them as she swallowed overcooked lamb. When Trecia offered a flat of bread, she instinctively ripped it in half, then remembered the words of Yeshua on the night He was betrayed, as had been recounted by those who reclined with Him. "Take; eat," He had said. "This is my body, broken for you."

At this thought, emotion gripped her heart again, torn between fear of what human beings were capable of doing and her incessant longing to please the One who had set her gloriously free from her previous life of idolatry. Though

Phoebe ate in silence, Trecia broke the quiet with her own words, chattering on and on about market prices, two lambs she met on the way with black faces, and the new weaving she was attempting to conquer. Words, words, words. While Trecia's words comforted her as the evening slipped into night, it was Paul's words that echoed through her thoughts when sleep eluded her.

Oh, dear Yeshua, what do You want me to do? I am afraid.

CHAPTER TWO

With the dawn came the weight of decision. The sunlight angling through the villa's *peristyle* seemed to confirm the inevitable. Phoebe had watched Paul labor over the scroll in question alongside a scribe, making the message succinct, powerful, and infused with the rhythms of the Holy Spirit. She knew the words like the lines of her right palm. Words about people turning astray to idols just as their fickle hearts had done in ancient Israel—worshipping false gods like Baal and Molech in a frenzy while God patiently pursued them. Shepherdlike. Her parents had chased the same wind, worshipping the created rather than the Creator. Blinded by sin and the cares of the world, they could not understand her heart, could not realize that following Jesus filled every crevice. Instead, they did as Jeremiah warned—dug for themselves broken cisterns that could hold no water, always trying to slake their thirst with mud, sticks, and stones.

It had been Phoebe and her dear husband, Albus, who prayed both their parents' mudslide of pursuit would end in surrender before God, but when Albus succumbed to the specter named Death, Phoebe faced everyone alone. Hers was a widowhood of completeness. Of utter aloneness, save Trecia's kindhearted service and friendship. When she bore the name

Widow, her eyes opened to those who bore the moniker without resource. She, a woman of means, did not have to worry about living well, but there were many, particularly in her congregation, whose days were marked by desperate gathering of resources, crumb by crumb. She'd considered it her primary calling from the Almighty when Albus died. To care for the widow and orphan in their distress.

Phoebe's hero? Stephen, the great martyr who never felt serving beneath his aspirations. It was told that when Stephen breathed his last, Jesus Christ stood to His feet at the right hand of God the Father to welcome him home. Phoebe determined to be like Stephen when she heard the story.

She sat up and breathed in a jasmine-scented morning, while Trecia's preparations for the morning meal in the villa's peristyle punctuated her thoughts. Who would take care of the widows if she traveled so far? What would happen if she never returned? How, then, would they live? Surely the Almighty would not ask such a thing. His heart beat with the cries of the broken, after all.

How big do you think I am?

The Spirit's words wrangled with her protests. She remembered the important truth that God still sat upon His throne while humanity slept. He worked while others idled. He consistently cared for pigeons, watering the wilderness unseen, seeing what no human could see. Greater than her greatest thought, God owned all the cattle, all the sheep, all the goats. He watered flowers whose faces never gazed on a person. He cared for His creation in its entirety, beyond borders, beyond seas, beyond imagination. All were laid bare before His loving gaze.

You are bigger than my biggest thought, she prayed.

I will take care of you, dear Phoebe. I only ask that you trust Me.

She placed her feet on the cool stone floor, felt its coolness shiver through her. "You, I trust. But what of this Joses? He is a stranger to me."

Her words floated onto the morning, while mourning doves sang and the Spirit kept His silence. Her heart, though, *knew.* She would leave everything behind and venture to Rome.

"We are taking a journey." Phoebe savored the yogurt and figs in front of her.

Trecia stopped and looked at her, must have felt the heaviness of the words that tumbled forth. "Where are we to go?"

"Rome."

With the word, Trecia uncharacteristically sat, a sigh heaving from her chest. "That will mean a sailing ship, will it not?"

Phoebe nodded.

"But my parents—"

"I know. Their demise is what makes this request so difficult." Phoebe touched Trecia's hand as a tear let loose and trailed down her maid's smooth face. "But the apostle Paul, he requested the journey. We are tasked with bringing the scroll to Priscilla and Aquila's church."

"Wherever you go," Trecia said, her voice wavering, "is where I go."

In the circle of their friendship, a community of two that weathered so much loss, quietness seeped into the moment while an errant fly dipped and buzzed around them, then landed on the yogurt. Trecia swatted the pest away, then pulled in another slow breath, exhaling what seemed to be the world's weight. There was much in that holy sigh, Phoebe knew. Fear. The unknown. The burden of God's scary call. The resolute decision to take a reckless journey alongside a friend. The hope of heaven. All of it—the tangle of nerves, the scent of adventure, the regret that would happen if they said no—permeated Phoebe.

She stood.

"We will go," she said.

CHAPTER THREE

In the atrium of her villa, Paul and Joses reclined, as if this were normal—that a leader of the known church and a relative stranger broke bread with a widow of means. "You understand the task?" Paul asked.

"It seems simple enough," Phoebe said. "Take this scroll to Rome to the house church there under Priscilla and Aquila's care. Walk to the port. Commission a ship to take us through three seas until we reach the shore west of Rome. Make our way to the city. Deliver the scroll." These points of travel had been her constant worry the past few weeks, as the sun rose and fell and she connected with people who could help her make the arduous journey. She secured a vessel set to embark in half a month's time, so they would need to leave soon.

"If only it were that simple." Joses rose. "There are dangers at every turn."

"Widowhood has made me strong," she said, but in her heart she knew the risks before them.

Joses held her gaze. "I have no doubt, but you may still need protection. The roads are haunted; the seas swell with raiders; the way to Rome is treacherous. I understand the way, have made it before. You need my eyes and wisdom."

She nearly dismissed him, but Paul's earnestness kept her silent.

He motioned for Joses to sit again. "Yes, yes, the journey. It will have its dangers—all of which I am aware of and have experienced. But no. There is more. You must understand the heart of my message. You must have the Gospel deeply woven into your mind. You must discern the reasons for my writing. And, ultimately, you must convey the meaning of its message to the hearers."

"Of course," Phoebe said.

Trecia entered the atrium, offering water to them all. She stood behind Phoebe.

Paul drank, emptying his cup, then pushing it heavenward toward Trecia to fill. He wiped his mouth after downing the next cup in the heat of the day. "No, you have to *read* the letter to them, inflecting my intentions. Yours is not merely a journey of means and danger, it is a task only halfway done when you find the Roman church. You must know it so well, know the Spirit behind it, that your words possess my urgency, my tone."

"Read the letter?" Phoebe swallowed. "As you would? But how can I do such a thing? I am not you. Your heart does not beat in my chest. Your mind does not inform mine. I am barely learned, unskilled in the world of words."

"Which is why it is you the Spirit has chosen," Paul said. "You are my friend. You have heard my dictation, how I paced the letter, how I informed the scribe. You have been with me throughout the entire scroll's message. You love Jesus as I do. And you have given your life for His Gospel. You have left all behind to follow Him, left your family, everything. Only someone who has sacrificed all can convey all."

Phoebe let Paul's words sink into her, let them bolster what little courage she felt in the moment. The air stilled. The voice of her Companion echoed, *by My strength, through My strength, with My strength alone.* "I will read the letter," she said.

"There is more." Paul nodded at Joses, whose eyes glinted as green as leaves. "This letter must be duplicated, many times, and delivered to the other brothers and sisters in Rome. This will take time and resources, Phoebe. So you see, once you arrive, *if* you arrive, Lord willing, you will not only read the scroll with my inflection, but you will also set out to hire scribes. This is a long work. It will not be fueled by youthful vigor or fleshly ambition. It will not succeed because of your ability. It will only move forward by the prompting and favor of the Spirit. He who goes behind, before, beside, will direct your moves." With this he looked at Trecia. "Are you a follower of Jesus?"

Trecia nodded but said nothing.

"Yes," Phoebe said. "When I met Him, our household met Him as well—just as the jailer's family bent to the will of God when he encountered Jesus after you and Silas miraculously escaped. As you know, it is common practice."

"Have I told you that story, Joses?" Paul shifted, his eyes glinting the way they did when a story played on his lips.

Joses shook his head. "No, Master, you have not."

"Call no man your master. Not anymore. You are freed in all ways by Christ."

At this Joses pulled his cloak around him as if cold—an anomaly for such a sweltering afternoon. A shadow seemed to cross over his face, then quickly dissipated.

Paul asked Trecia to sit with them. She declined and continued to stand. "Silas and I sat in prison for preaching the Way in the city of Philippi. The Spirit had given us favor when we went to the place of prayer outside the city gate. There, we met Lydia."

"Is she the woman who reminded you of me?" Phoebe asked.

"Yes, a woman of strength. A woman of prayer. A woman of means. A woman who opened her heart to the One who fashioned her heart. My own heart thrilled as we shared the Good News with her." He nodded to Trecia. "Her household entrusted themselves to Jesus as well."

"Did they have any choice?" Joses's voice was low, resonating from somewhere strong within him.

"This is a mystery," Paul said. "Who God calls, who responds—but what I know to the midst of my soul is that once someone meets Jesus Christ, the air shivers and shifts, the world's light changes from shadows to light, and a child is born into newness. Everything that marked their past becomes rubbish, and the future splays before them brightly, invigorated by the unearned love of God."

Phoebe wondered how she could possibly convey the passion of this man to people she had never met. Could she read his letter with similar verve?

"Your story," Trecia prompted.

"Yes. Lydia embraced the Good News. But alas, there's always a trickster at work, isn't there?"

"How so?" Joses asked.

"You must understand this." Paul stood, then paced the courtyard. For a long time he did not speak, and as he waited, it seemed to Phoebe that everyone held their collective breaths. Finally Paul said, "Whenever there is a great work of God afloat, the enemy of our souls will be sure to interfere. And it is never the same way twice. Remember this, all of you."

Trecia simply nodded, her face solemn.

"An interloper of Satan followed after us. Constantly. Like a drip of water never ceasing. It stole the words of a young slave girl and oddly spoke the truth. She said, 'These men are servants of the Most High God, who are proclaiming to you the way of salvation.'"

"What is wrong with that?" Phoebe shifted. "Aren't those the same words you have spoken to the church here—the way of salvation?"

"Yes, but they were spoken in a tortuous loop from the mouth of a medium—a genuine blasphemy, a mockery of the goodness of God. Finally Silas and I grew exasperated after days of her verbal singsong. I turned to face her and then said, 'In the name of Jesus Christ I command you to come out of her.' The spirit could not stand against that beautiful name, and it slipped out."

"This is good news, is it not?" Joses smiled.

"For the girl, yes," Paul said. "But for her handlers who made money from her clairvoyance? Not good. We cut the knees out from under their financial security. Without demonic powers, this girl roamed free, but she no longer made her owners any money. You can imagine the fury that ensued."

Paul leaned against a wall, traced his hands along the stones. "The men dragged Silas and me before the magistrate and accused us of throwing their city into turmoil—that we were undermining Rome's authority. The crowd lent their voices to the chaos, demanding our backs. The officials, more concerned with crowds than justice, ordered us stripped, then beaten with rods. Which is where our jailer enters the story. He had been tasked with leading us to the inner part of the prison, then fastened our feet in stocks."

Phoebe tried to imagine such a thing—to be stripped, beaten, imprisoned in the bowels of such a dark place. She could feel Trecia's tension behind her, no doubt thinking the same thing: *this could be us.*

Joses crossed powerful arms over himself. "You are here, and we know the jailer's fate, but I must admit, this story has me fretting. It seems impossible to remedy."

"That it was," Paul said. "But we serve a God of impossibilities. Silas and I knew this. Yet we both considered it the highest privilege to suffer for our Savior, so midnight found us praying earnest prayers for deliverance, while singing hymns of praise for who God is. We remembered the story of the fiery furnace from days of old where one like a son of man danced in the midst of people untouched by flame. Nothing, nothing is impossible for our God. But our hearts were full nonetheless. It was precisely in the midst of our revelry of our Savior that the foundations of the earth shook us utterly free. The stocks fell away, suddenly broken. The doors rattled open, and we walked out free."

"And the jailer?" Joses leaned toward Paul, as if straining to hear.

"He begged us, 'What must I do to be saved?' He began his evening enslaving us, but he ended in dawn's light as a freed man. He collapsed before the power of Jesus and then allowed us to share the Good News with his household. His was a reformation of self, then family and community. He salved the wounds he inflicted, fed us a feast, and then Silas and I baptized the entire household."

"And what of the officials? What did they say?" Phoebe asked.

"They wanted us to slip away, but through the jailer we conveyed that we were Roman citizens, which alarmed them greatly. In the end, we visited Lydia, strengthened her, and then we left the city." Paul quieted and walked back to the place he once reclined. He looked at Phoebe, eyes ablaze. "This will be the markings of your journey. There will be confusion, pain, exasperation—as all good adventures with the Spirit have. But as things grow dark as night, may you find yourself praying and praising. When all seems lost and impossible, remember the privilege it is to suffer for the Almighty One, then praise Him, praise Him, praise Him. He will be with you. He will never forsake you, Phoebe."

She swallowed. Felt Paul's words in her soul. The peace of the Lord flowed through her, from within to without. "We will set out as soon as we can," she said.

CHAPTER FOUR

Far too much preparation to make such a hasty vow. Phoebe tasted the bitterness of the haste as she prepared, hoping Paul would not count her enthusiasm against her. She knew the importance of the mission, the beauty of the scroll she would carry.

Trecia busied herself with curating provisions—dried meat, fruit, olives—anything that would not spoil under the sun. She gathered tunics, stolas, and *pallas* for both shade and warmth. Phoebe knew her reticence, but her friend hummed as she worked, though fear tinged each melody.

The slap of sandals upon cobble kept the household humming, while Phoebe nursed a headache and the vestiges of a queasy stomach. Were her insides predicting what would happen upon the seas once they departed the safety of Cenchreae? Would the waves roil her resolve? Would the sea become her grave marker? With the passing of Albus, life felt more frail, as fragile as a winter blossom poking its expectant head one moment, wilting beneath the cold the next. Life held no guarantees, she knew. And life in the Spirit? She could not say where the wind would take her next, or whether this voyage would be her last. Part of her relished the possibility of her passing from life to death to life. Did not Paul say that to live was Christ, but to die was to gain yet more of Him? But there was the human side of her, the part that deeply enjoyed the ministry God had graciously given her here—families in crisis; the poor who needed food, shelter, and love; the church in want of administration and funding—this was the side that felt dread down to her bones. She wondered who would fill her sandals here if those sandals sunk to the depths of the seas.

I am God. You are not.

"Yes," she said to the busy courtyard.

And at the moment, Trecia mentioned that Paul and Joses had arrived without invitation.

"Invite them in." She hoped her voice did not hint at exasperation.

Paul carried two scrolls as Joses walked behind him. "Let us recline," he said. And they did, beside the impluvium. Paul thanked Trecia, and she left the room.

"These are your treasures, Phoebe." Paul placed the scrolls between them.

"Why two?" Phoebe remembered the length of the letter to the Roman believers. It stretched a courtyard long, but it had not been dissected.

Paul pointed to the seal of the one to her left. "This one is the letter." He traced his fingers over the scroll, caressing it as a man is wont to do when he touches his greatest work. His hair, now grown out from, perhaps, an unspoken vow, caught the sun's light.

She could see silver threading its way through—each gray hair earned by his continued burden of carrying the weight of every single church he had planted. The complications troubled his thoughts, she knew. And his dictation of letters gave her insight to the heart of this father of churches. He loved them all, she knew.

"And this other?" Joses asked.

Phoebe could not read the look on Joses's face, as they had barely been acquainted over the past week. But something lived behind those eyes, some story untold, a map of mistrust?

"This is precisely how to locate Priscilla and Aquila's tent-making business. It is where they work, live, and host their church. It is not easy to find, and you must not lose this scroll."

"They look identical," Phoebe said. "How will we know which is which?"

On the corner of the exposed end of one scroll, Paul pointed to a small smudge of ink, barely noticeable. "Joses, Phoebe, you must memorize this." Paul's voice sounded pinched, almost panicked. "You will need both these scrolls to accomplish the mission the Lord Jesus has called you to."

"But sir," Joses said, "what if—"

"God will go with you, and He will make your footfalls firm. The Spirit will guide you to the place He wants this message. Your occupation is to trust. And to worship. And to trust some more. This is not your journey, it is His." Paul stood, while the scrolls remained. "Let us go, Joses." And so the two men left, leaving Phoebe alone with treasure—one a treasure of Gospel words, the other a treasure of Gospel people. Both precious. Both necessary. Both beautiful.

She gathered them to herself as Trecia entered.

"Is that the letter?" Trecia asked.

"Yes," Phoebe said. "We must keep it safe."

"It will be my greatest privilege to do so. Wait there a moment," Trecia said.

While a bee hummed around the tangle of roses nearby, Trecia left then returned with a leather satchel deep enough to pocket the scrolls. "Place them here."

Phoebe obeyed and then said, "Blessed be the God and Father of our Lord Jesus Christ. May He protect us, preserve this letter, and bring us to those who need Paul's words. May we be considered faithful, available for service. May He complete what He began, that the journey that begins with one step ends successfully on the roads of Rome. All through the power of the Holy Spirit, I pray."

"Amen." Trecia smiled, then took the leather bag to be packed.

CHAPTER FIVE

The morning glistened after the rain, the streets resembling the gold of the New Heavens and New Earth Paul espoused. And there he stood, beneath the roses, his eyes unreadable, Joses beside him. The three of them, Phoebe, Trecia, and Joses would make an odd traveling party, but their completion was the Spirit who lived in them all, who would make their pathway straight.

"Before you leave, I have a gift," Paul said. He held nothing in his hand, no extra provisions, no financial remuneration. Empty-handed, yet expectant.

"Thank you." Phoebe shifted her weight, wondering how her sandals would withstand the rocky streets as they ventured to the port.

At that, Paul laughed, deep, guttural, joyful. He looked into Phoebe's eyes. Theirs was a familial friendship—nothing more, the kind of love a brother and sister curated over a shared history of heartache. They had endured the difficulties of people and ministry together. They bore scars and war wounds, though he had far more. She had yet to be beaten for her beliefs, left for dead, smuggled over city walls, flogged. A scar marred Paul's left cheek—a tattoo of valor for all he suffered. She wanted to touch it, though propriety held her back. "You, unlike your traveling companions, have heard the entirety of the message. You know its contents, nearly by heart, I hope."

"This is true." Phoebe swallowed, remembering the labor of words. She nearly choked back tears, realizing in this present moment what it all meant. This could be their last shred of friendship—this goodbye under a now cloudless sky. If she said the ominous words out loud, surely Paul would laugh and assure her of the great hereafter, that goodbyes on earth were simply precursors, to greetings in that pristine place. For the Christ follower, goodbye rent the heart, but it could not cut clear through. Hope infused every interaction, every moment. It could not help but break through—even in tragedy.

"But there is more. You were not there for its final rendering, the place where I offer greetings, commendations."

"I did not realize there was more," Phoebe said.

"Yes, you will read it aloud in Rome, but there are a few sentences I want you to know before you leave today." Paul cleared his throat, took in a halcyon breath, smiled, and then said, "'I commend to you our sister Phoebe, who is a deacon in the church in Cenchreae. Welcome her in the Lord as one who is worthy of honor among God's people. Help her in whatever she needs, for she has been helpful to many, and especially to me.'" With this, his bright eyes glistened.

"I do not know what to say." Phoebe knew Paul to be a man of few words when it came to commending others. Often his words were measured for those falling away in apostasy or wrangling unnecessarily over minutia or living as ravenous wolves in a sheep's deceptive clothing. She felt his words permeate her, as honey to her bitterness, fresh wellspring water for the dry years after Albus died. They were light and life, as if God Himself had taken note of her as He did Hagar in the wilderness—the God who saw her. Noticed. Commended.

"The words are true," Paul said. "You are a sister to the sisterless, a helper among the believers, a woman of valor and honor, and most of all—a dear, dear friend." He grabbed her hands, kissed each palm, and nodded. He let her hands drop, then turned to Joses. "Take care of her as if she were a treasure buried in a field. She is a sister of light, and she is taking on this journey with the fear of the Lord as her companion."

"It is my delight to protect her," Joses said. But he avoided Phoebe's gaze.

"Trecia, serve Phoebe well, will you?"

Trecia took Phoebe's hand. "It is my honor to do so."

"Let me pray," Paul said. They gathered around while the morning's coolness slipped toward warmth. "These, Your servants, are partnering with me in the sharing of Your great Gospel, Lord. They carry words of life, truth, rebuke, and encouragement. I pray for safety of passage, protection from storms both natural and human, and opportunities to share You with those who are dying without hope. May this voyage widen the tent pegs of Your kingdom, Jesus. May their love overflow. Infuse this journey with Your joy, Lord Jesus Christ, and remind them of the privilege it is to suffer for Your sake. Protect them from the spiritual forces of evil in this world, from their adversary, Satan, who roars but has no bite. Lead them. Guide them. Restore them when they're weak. In difficulties, give them Your perspective. Amen and amen."

Phoebe choked out an amen. She heard Joses's throaty amen echo behind her. As the three gathered their provisions and made their way toward the port, she told herself not to be like Lot's wife, but her heart would not obey.

She turned back.

There stood Paul like a pillar, unmoving and steadfast, though his shoulders slumped ever so slightly. He nodded her way, then turned, pacing back toward the work God called him to do—to fashion tents and make disciples. It would be a long time before she felt sheltered, she knew. But with each step, the Holy Spirit sang hope through her.

I will not leave you.

CHAPTER SIX

The three trailed through a spot of relative wilderness, saying nothing—a quiet triad of introspection, Phoebe thought. The trees above swayed to the rhythm of her breath while her sandals beat a cadence on the road beneath her feet. She felt a blister take shape in her left arch. While she had been full of zeal for the adventure ahead, she now faced the reality of a long journey where enthusiasm waned.

"How long until we reach the port?" Trecia sheltered her eyes from the sun, straining beneath her hand-tent toward the eastern horizon. The sun shone hot from the top of the world, spotlighting them beneath its gaze.

Perspiration trailed down the back of Phoebe's too-hot tunic.

"Five good hours of walking from plain to port," Joses said, laughter just beneath his voice. "You sound like a child I once knew, always wanting to get to a place, seldom enjoying the adventure of the walk." With this, the stranger-to-them pointed out the flora and fauna around them, naming birds by the sounds of their calls, the specific type of grapevine scrabbling up a stone wall, why that insect seemed to walk backward, and precisely how long it would be until the sun dipped below the horizon.

"You like to talk."

"Just passing the time." He whistled for a few strides, then looked at her. "Stories of what we see keep us occupied, help us forget the heat, the blisters, the worry, don't you think?"

"I agree," Trecia said. "Don't stop. I am learning. This trip is my liberation, my education. I have not left the confines of Cenchreae, have not understood the ways of the world beyond front doors, city gates. The shoreline is the farthest I have ventured. But you? You have been many places, is that right?"

Joses sighed, rubbed his calloused hands together. "More than many. In a way I have lived three men's lives. I am grateful to have the chance for yet one more life. Paul has given me wings."

His words disrupted a gaggle of geese to their right who suddenly took flight, flapping, honking, soaring, seemingly unaffected by the sun's permanence.

"They sound like laughter," Trecia said.

"Yes, or a roomful of conversation." Joses stopped, then watched the fowl fly clear away, his hand shading his eyes.

As they started forward after the geese ovation, Phoebe felt hunger rumble within.

"Let us sit a moment and eat," Joses offered. "Shade beckons." And beckon it did. A stand of leafy trees swayed from the warm breeze, with three sturdy stumps beneath—a banquet hall of nature.

"I am hungry," Trecia said, voicing Phoebe's rumblings.

They ate in silence, as Phoebe tried to envision what they would face. It was the not knowing that knotted her stomach. And yet Paul's strong confidence in her and her companions settled some of the murmurings within.

CHAPTER SEVEN

Hours later, feet forlorn and bleeding from the soles, Phoebe arrived at the pristine harbor with Trecia and Joses. It stretched before them like a promise, crescent shaped and aquamarine. Many sailing ships, masts pointing toward the now-forming clouds, rocked back and forth in the cove, a natural haven. The sun sank behind them, casting the late afternoon in dusk. Motes of dust frolicked in the pristine light. But weariness settled into Phoebe as she scanned the seaport. "Let us go there." She pointed at a stand of vessels. "Our ship is among those."

Upon arrival, the cacophony of voices threatened to drown hers. Ropes hurled between vessel and dock. Cargo passed from man to man. Sails scrubbed and rerigged. Everyone seemed to be rushing here and there, with no leader to direct their frenetic activity.

Phoebe touched the cloak of a young man. "I am looking for Cadmus the sailor."

"Sorry, ma'am. But that ship has departed. Must have been during the second hour the sails erected, and off she went."

"But that was our ship, the one I commissioned." Phoebe pulled out a small scroll that indicated the transaction. "Right here."

"I cannot read, ma'am," the boy said. "But, here, I will take you to one who can." He snaked through a jostling crowd while the three companions followed. "Here he is. This is Regulus. He is the captain of the *Paralus*." He pointed to the group. "I am sorry. I did not ask your names in my haste."

Phoebe approached the man named Regulus. "I am Phoebe of Corinth. I chartered a vessel to take my companions and myself to Rome, via Cadmus. Do you know this Cadmus?"

Regulus stood a head taller than Phoebe. He eyed Joses with suspicion. "Do I know you? You have a familiarity about you."

Joses shifted before him. "No, I do not believe so, sir. I am not from this port."

"Very well." He kept his eyes on Joses, but the freed slave looked away. "Now to address the captain you hired. Yes, I do know Cadmus, but he is not a worthwhile man."

Phoebe wanted to say *obviously*, but she kept her tongue captive. "He has taken payment in *aureus* already." She heard tears in her voice, but she withheld them. It would do her no good to weep before the stranger.

Regulus frowned. "Unfortunately, this type of transaction is his specialty. His words are as slick as his promises. Which is why he hastily departs prior to posted departure times. His is a life of constant swindling, then fleeing, I'm afraid." He cleared his throat, then spat upon the ground.

Phoebe hopped backward to avoid the spittle.

Trecia shrieked, but Phoebe touched her hand and whispered for her to calm herself.

"It is not kind to do such a vulgar thing," Joses said.

"Well, this is not the best environment for the faint of heart." With this, Regulus looked square into Phoebe's face. "Ships have a way of swallowing the vulnerable. The boats will rock your stomach clear inside out, blue your lips, and in the inevitable storm, leviathan may just leap to the deck and swallow you clear up." He laughed, throaty and long. His smile bore mismatched teeth, some missing, some blackened by time. And his breath smelled of rotting fish. "You have learned an important lesson, ma'am."

Anger replaced any fear that knotted her stomach. "I am not *ma'am*. I am a woman called by God on a mission to Rome. I am not without means. You would do well to listen. I have found that *denarii* are no respecter of persons. Whether it comes from the hand of a woman, a slave, a scoundrel—it still holds its value."

Regulus stepped backward as darkness began to rise on the eastern horizon. "Now, do not take me for a fool. I just happen to be traveling Rome's way this very night. I have scant room, though. You will have to hole up in a storage bunk—all three of you."

"I will sleep upon the deck," Joses offered. "I like the freedom of the stars, the open air, if that is amenable to you, Regulus."

"Of course, and we could use a back as strong as yours. Perhaps payment can be reduced for your agreement of labor. What say you?"

"I am accustomed to work, and anything to lighten our burden is my privilege." He looked Phoebe's way and nodded at Trecia. "As long as you promise their safety."

Regulus nodded. "I swear by the great sea, they will be safe."

They agreed on a price while Joses set to haul their belongings toward the *Paralus*. Phoebe clutched the leather satchel to herself, however. She would be the keeper of this treasure. As Paul entrusted it to her, she would entrust it to no one but herself.

"What do you have here, Phoebe?" Regulus touched the satchel, his fingers tinged with grease and blood.

Phoebe recoiled from his touch, scanning the crowd for a hopefully returning Joses, and then inwardly scolded herself for needing someone. Hadn't she survived the trial of widowhood sufficiently? "A lady needs some secrets, does she not?"

"I have found secrets to be burdensome." With this, Regulus turned toward the ship, and left her and Trecia alone, yet buffeted in the midst of a burgeoning crowd.

"I am afraid." Trecia moved toward the ship, then stopped. "I am afraid of death upon the seas."

For a moment, Phoebe thought of a lecture to perform—of trust, fearlessness, and believing God to be on their side, but all her words jumbled in the reality of what they both faced— an unknown voyage, an unsavory captain, an unstable sea, an enigmatic protector. Wind that once cooled her face now frenzied, as if to answer her fears with vengeance. "I understand," she said. Because she did. Paul often spoke of an ironic peace that God gave in the midst of tumult, and she begged the Spirit to grant her such tranquility, but her stomach's shifting mimicked the flapping of the giant sail before her—back and forth, unstable, moved by an unseen hand. Phoebe calculated their remaining funds and worried. This second commissioning of a vessel certainly drained them to the bare bones of provision.

Trecia grabbed Phoebe's elbow just as rain pelted the earth. "Best we take cover on the ship."

They ran to the rhythm of the rain as it soaked Phoebe to the skin. She thanked the Lord that the satchel repelled water, keeping the precious scrolls safe and dry. But as they picked their way over the narrow bridge to the *Paralus*, lightning illuminated the ricketiness of the vessel. Rotting fish strewed the upper deck. Men of glinting eyes and no-doubt ill intentions eyed them both. The boat's deck was slick with something Phoebe could not place, though its smell reminded her of the acrid smoke of burning waste. *What have we done?*

Stemming Phoebe's rising panic, Joses appeared like a savior, ushering them both beneath the deck via an unstable ladder extended into the ship's belly.

Trecia's foot slipped, and she pummeled to the inner deck below. She called out, shrieking.

Phoebe hushed her as several sailors turned toward them, eyes hungry. "Can you get to your feet?"

She nodded, then hobbled her way toward a rickety doorway. "I want to go home," she said.

"We must face this journey with bravery," Phoebe whispered.

Trecia cried but attempted to silence herself. Instead, her waist and shoulders shook, while she gulped in several breaths beneath her palla.

"Steady now," Joses said. He pointed to the doorway. "This is where you will stay," he said, a hint of sadness in his voice.

Behind the doorway the stench permeated Phoebe's resolve. She told her stomach to steady and then instinctively pinched her nose with her right hand. "What is this place?"

"Seems to be where vermin go to die," Joses said. "It is still not too late to disembark and try for another vessel. Perhaps a cleaner one?"

Phoebe remembered Paul's intent, his desire, the words he painstakingly communicated to a church she had never seen. She tried to imagine the faces of those who worshipped God in danger, hungry for encouragement, in need of guidance and wisdom. She touched the satchel, then straightened herself. "No. We will continue. Ten days at sea—is that not the standard time of the voyage?"

Joses nodded. "But ten days at sea are not the same as ten on earth."

"Surely we can tarry ten days," Phoebe said. "What is ten days in light of eternity?"

"You shall soon find out." His voice sounded ominous as the rain continued its relentless pursuit of the vessel. It thrummed a steady beat above their heads, while leaks splattered the dark, ominous-smelling room—if you could call it that. More like a tiny prison.

"You will not stay with us?" Trecia asked.

"It would not be proper, but I will sleep exactly above you. I will rap upon your roof, to let you know of my presence. If you need anything, or danger comes near, knock on the ceiling, and I will descend and help you. I am serious. Do you understand?"

Phoebe nodded. But the darkness meant Joses would not see such a response.

"Do you understand?" he pleaded.

"Yes, I understand," Phoebe finally said. "If trouble comes, we will knock. Do not worry yourself about us. We have been companions many years, and we know how to keep warm in dark situations, is not that right, Trecia?"

"Yes," she said. But her voice betrayed any sort of confidence that word was intended to convey.

Joses took his leave of them. In the dark, Phoebe pulled a woolen stola around them both as they shivered beneath the relentless drip from above. She remembered Paul's story of prison and the jailer—an impossible situation to remedy—and she began to sing. Hymns of praise. Snippets of psalms memorized, declarations of faith that sounded grandiose but failed to rise to the height of faith when they escaped her lips. Trecia failed to join in as her teeth chattered. Still, Phoebe persisted, hoping for a miracle.

"I want to sleep," Trecia said. "Would you stop singing?"

In that hiccup of a request, Phoebe felt suddenly alone. She had experienced a quiet revelry in her singing, a pinch of hope as she lifted her voice heavenward. But her melody, one she momentarily thought sacred, was simply an annoyance— to her closest companion. *Lord, is this the smallest bit of what You felt like in the garden? Alone? Forgive me; I don't presume to understand the magnitude of what You suffered.* She sighed at the thought. But then she remembered the words of her friend Paul—that it was a divine privilege to suffer for the sake of the One who suffered everything. That in following Jesus down the exceedingly narrow path, she would be completing the suffering of Christ. Her pain would matter. It would usher in a deep camaraderie as she suffered alongside the Suffering Servant. Paul had called it a privilege. Jesus continued to suffer for His bride, the Church, and when those who loved Him suffered for the good of the Church, they found companionship. To suffer alongside Christ was the greater privilege, she knew. And as the drips permeated her scalp and ran tears down her face, she felt suddenly warmed at the thought. As her eyes felt heavy with the thought of sleep, a simple rapping above her—*knock, knock, knock*—reminded her of Joses's promise kept.

CHAPTER EIGHT

Light swirled around Phoebe in a rainbow dance. Was this heaven? Albus now stood before her in their atrium, his once sallow skin pink. He winked at her, their secret sign. "This is an important journey," he told her. "Your strength must be large, though the dangers loom."

She tried to open her mouth in reply, but as in the maddening effect of dreams, she could not utter a word. She tried to close the distance between them but found her feet to be clay stuck to the cobble. Unmovable, like a statue carved in ivory. And in a wink of the moment, Albus sat, then lay prostrate upon the floor. His life drained from him, like a pitcher poured water, while his pink complexion grayed and breathing ceased.

She awoke in the darkness while Trecia lightly snored. Through the planks above, she could see small rectangles of sky—a promise that the earth still existed as it had before this journey. While gazing through the transom-like openings where Joses most likely slept, she allowed herself a moment of remembrance, tracing the hand of God from childhood to this very place. All seemed light and beauty in the courtyard of her youth. Her parents spent their lives loving her—a contrast to those around her who viewed children as livestock, workhorses whose job it was to provide for their parents. No, her parents asked questions, educated her, doted on her with affection. The shift had not subtly happened until that summer evening so many years ago—what seemed like a lifetime.

Their first encounter happened in a Corinthian manner, at the shrine dedicated to Asklepios, the god of healing, where people bustled about with clay renderings of what, exactly, needed to be attended to by the god. Albus's carving was that of a left foot, as his trailed dumbly behind him, as if its energy had drained clear out. Desperate to be whole, Albus placed his terra cotta offering on the shrine's steps, then limped backward, tripping over Phoebe. He steadied himself by grabbing her arm. Phoebe cried out, but once she saw the man's predicament, she apologized.

"You need healing?" she asked.

Albus limped backward, hands raised toward the shrine's pinnacle. "I am sorry. This foot—it does not cooperate, even under the gaze of the gods. I have brought many offerings here, but it seems the gods are unseeing to my plight."

There was something in his eyes, the steady, earnest gaze he gave that seemed reserved for her alone. His was an unashamed need, a willingness to be humble and honest about a foot that would not walk right. She felt his words, his predicament in her heart. "I hope you gain what you are seeking," she said.

"Your name?" he asked.

"I am Phoebe."

"Albus." He genuflected ever so slightly in a manner that made her laugh. "I am afraid all I have to offer you is my sense of humor about life's inconveniences."

Such a simple first conversation—just a few words, really. But their encounter disrupted everything normal. Phoebe, promised in marriage to another, could not shake this man with his wounded foot. He haunted her, coerced her train of thought. And as they formed a friendship—something others frowned upon—she realized she had a heroic task before her, to convince her parents of Albus's virtue.

When he stood, bent-footed, to be her husband, she beamed at the luck of the gods to have arranged such a union. Though it had been near impossible, her father and mother who desperately loved her, agreed to the match after dissolving the more prudent familial one—the opportune family connection that would have doomed her to servitude and sadness. Joy raced through her as Albus touched her cheek, promising the gods the world.

They created their own world, the two of them. All carefully planned through commerce and guts and hard work until the gods granted success despite Albus's inwardly turned foot. The sun shone. The world applauded. The bronze *asses*, then silver denarii, then the golden *aureus* made their way into their satchels—thanks to so many seafaring men in want of supplies.

But her womb? It never answered back, as lame as Albus's foot. And in that despair, they found themselves carving the image of a baby into an earthen pot, returning to the Asklepios shrine to pay their respects as Albus had done innumerable times. Why they did that, Phoebe did not know. Albus's foot remained unhealed, after all. But a desperate womb is hungry—it cries for filling, so they climbed in dutiful obedience, placed the offering, and meandered home, sorrow permeating them both. It hugged them in impenetrable fog but seldom evaporated.

Theirs was no Damascus road. Theirs was a happenstance meeting with a simple woman whose name is recorded in the Book of Life but otherwise unremarkable. She emerged as if from nowhere on their pathway of sorrow, stout and hunched. She pointed an arthritic finger their way, wagged it like a small dog's tail. "It is useless," she said.

Phoebe felt those three words jab her heart. These words were true. She felt them like weariness as they presented the clay pot, a simple vessel of earth. How could carving a request matter to an indifferent, capricious god? How many pieces of earthenware littered the shrine, representing unmet expectations, ruined hopes, and unanswered requests? Thousands, many of which had been cracked and decaying at her feet, heaped like unanswered prayers. Shattered as much as her dreams for a baby had become. She said nothing to the woman at first as grief thickened her tongue.

The old woman touched her right shoulder and Albus's left, pushing them together on that narrow road—as if they were bride and groom and she the officiate. "You two will no longer be forsaken," she said. "The One who made your foot, your womb, your lives, your union is not a god who is far off. He is the One who created you from your mothers' wombs. He has allowed you to exhaust all piety at the threshold of little gods that have no breath, no mouth, no eyes, certainly no heart. Today is the day you will finally see the truth."

Albus melted under the woman's touch, falling to his knees, eyes spilling the tears of a lifetime. "I am undone," he said.

Something akin to love welled up inside Phoebe then, but not from herself. It was not pity, this love. No, it poured from without, from a greater vessel to a lesser, a river of love that she had spent a lifetime thirsting for. "What is this?"

"Jesus Christ, the Son of God," the woman said plainly. "He is who is healing you, leading you to a new path, a river of life. You will no longer be called forsaken, but chosen. You will reap a new family as you turn your life over to the One who died on your behalf." The woman continued to share what she called Good News as the afternoon spent itself, and they found some rounded rocks to sit upon. She placed her shaking hand upon Albus's foot, invoking the name of Jesus, speaking of the power of what she called a Holy Spirit, and in an instant, Albus shot up, leaping upon the once-lame foot.

Phoebe's heart leapt too, to the rhythm of his dance. What kind of god cared enough to do such a thing? What kind of magic was this? It felt ancient, yet as tangible as human touch.

After Albus finally wearied from the dance on his new foot, the woman beckoned them both as she spoke of a nation called Israel, of prophets, of a stubborn people and their bent toward violating a covenant. Her eyes lit when she introduced Jesus, the One sent from God to make all things right. He too healed the lame, the lost, the broken, the barren. He stooped to hear the cries of the ones cast out by such predicaments and ailments. And when the religious elite felt threatened and jealous, they put Jesus to death on a horrid cross. Phoebe had unfortunately seen a crucifixion once, and shuddered to think such a holy Man could endure such agony. At this point in her storytelling, the woman winked at Phoebe. "Do you want to know what happened next?"

Phoebe nodded.

"He had foretold what would happen, but His voice was echoed by many before Him—prophets of old who saw with the eyes of seers that the One who would reconcile the world to a Holy God would suffer to do so. That is the meaning of sacrifice—that it costs a person. But then!" At this she stood, waving that crooked finger again, but with the glint of eye that shone like the ripples of the sea. "Three days after darkness, light rose. He conquered death! He rose from the grave!"

Phoebe had heard rumors of this Jesus, particularly followers of what was called the Way. She had casually dismissed such fanatic devotion, but in light of her husband's healed foot and the earnestness of the woman's storytelling, she felt inexplicably drawn to the narrative. And that is when the Spirit of God invaded afresh.

She wept. Every pain, every worry, every unspoken fear welled up from within and spilled out of her while the very presence of God swirled around them both. Confession could not help but pour forth. Laid bare, broken, unnerved, they continued to speak to the One who reversed their plight, who welcomed them into His family. Neither of them noticed that the woman who had brought such revolution disappeared. In one moment they came to themselves in that circle of three to find it had dissipated to two. They sat on two rocks, the third abandoned. And they wondered. And wept. And laughed.

When they stood, both on steady feet, neither realized the shift that occurred—that their trajectory was completely altered, utterly changed. Soon they would find a small group of believers who followed the Way, and their tidy world would shatter apart under the accusations of everyone who had loved them well. The pivot happened swiftly, Phoebe saw now. And that was when the childlike trust in her parents diminished, slowly replaced by the true family of God. She'd been abandoned by one family to be grafted into another. And dear Trecia, her sister in Christ who now breathed the foul air in and out beside her, stayed with her through it all. Albus, whose perfectly beautiful foot remained healed, succumbed to a wasting disease as if one ailment had been violently exchanged for a deadlier one, leaving her bereft, abandoned.

Here she sat, cramped and sequestered beneath a sail bent toward a city she had never been to, desperately trying to remind herself of the faithfulness of God that had brought her thus far. It was not carved on earthen pottery but upon her heart. He who was the potter, she the clay, would bring her safely to the harbor, she hoped. She prayed, thanking God again for the unnamed woman who dared to risk everything on that fading afternoon road. When she'd told the Corinthian church of the woman, she expected them all to nod, to recount their own stories of surprising encounters, but none could. This woman, was she an angel? Something imagined?

No, she had been flesh and blood. Phoebe could remember the warmth of her wrinkled hand, the glint in her eyes, the way in which her voice wavered with excitement every time she mentioned Jesus's name. She had been as real as the ship that now rocked her. As real as the discarded clay pots on the shrine's hillside. As real as Albus's healing. As real as the apostle Paul's earnest request. This, she knew.

The old woman had fulfilled a divine mission. And now Phoebe had been tasked with another one. She pulled in a reeking breath, telling herself not to vomit. She crouched, then stood in the hollow of the small room, choosing to venture up the ladder toward the skyline. Dawn greeted her with hazy clouds and the dull gray of lifting fog. She pulled her palla around herself and relished a moment alone while the wind whipped through her. She could no longer see the land, and felt utterly solitary. The horizon rollicked before her. Seawater sprayed her cheeks at the precise moment her tears erupted, both salted. She thought of the disciples, themselves storm tossed and frightened, how they called out to Jesus for rescue. He had stood, settling the waves and sea as if a trifle of insignificance. Surely He could bring peace in her storm.

"Oh, dear Jesus," she said into the wind. "If You could silence the storm clouds, my tears seem small by comparison. Bring me safely to Rome, I ask."

A hand upon her shoulder startled her. She reeled around to see Joses, eyes fixed ahead. "You should not be up here. It is no place for a woman."

"Where else am I supposed to be?" She tried to tame the edge that had crept into her voice, but their circumstances had coaxed her mood. "I am sorry," she said.

Joses shook his head, as if he both understood her shortness and felt the weight of their predicament all at once. He looked at her with concern. "I have been tasked to protect you, and this is not a safe place." He darted his eyes toward several sailors to his left, who leered at her. "Please heed my counsel, Phoebe. You will make my task easier if you do."

She cast a glance toward the group of men. Fear grabbed at her then. She nodded at Joses, swallowing her worry, then descended the ladder.

She woke up Trecia. "We should eat something," she said.

CHAPTER NINE

The first day at sea began with promise. The sun kissed the sail while winds blessed the vessel westward. Phoebe and Trecia picked their way along the merchant ship's spine where the mast soared to the sky and secured a place for themselves toward the rear of the vessel. Joses labored nearby, scrubbing the deck, while perspiration reeked through his outer tunic. With the sun indicating midday, he joined Phoebe and Trecia for a small meal of dried figs and unleavened bread while they passed a skin of water between them.

"You look exhausted," Phoebe said.

"Alas, yes, it is so." Joses took a long drink. "My body begs for work, it seems. Ever since I was a boy, I had a back made to bend, arms to lift, legs to work. Sometimes I feel like a horse in service of others."

Trecia tore a piece of bread and handed it to him. "But you are free now."

Joses said nothing, but he smiled while he put up his hand. "Best save the provisions. I am used to deprivations, having trained myself to work without food for many days. One never knows the fickleness of ships. We may yet need this food in the coming days."

Phoebe shielded her eyes from the relentless sun. On days like today it seemed an impossibility that the sun would ever cease its shining. "I believe God smiles upon this voyage."

"If that is what you say." Joses drank again. "But we must remember that those who follow the Way have the inevitability of trials and tribulations. They are our passageways to enter the narrow kingdom. Let us not think that everything will be easy sailing."

"You are borrowing trouble with your words, Joses." Phoebe ate a fig, cherishing the sweetness on her tongue.

"And you are ignoring its possibility." Joses stood.

Trecia laughed. "Let us not argue. Bantering wastes the beauty of today. I, for one, intend on reveling in the light, grateful for the calm."

"And I will work till dusk." Joses returned to his duty, but Phoebe noticed that darkness had swept over his face.

A young man with wild eyes and small stature approached Trecia. "It is not often we sailors have female company on a voyage," he said.

Phoebe felt his words, knew the tenor of a voice like that. She placed her hand on Trecia's leg. "Have you met our companion Joses?" She pointed toward the hardworking man whose back bent beneath a load he carried.

"Yes, yes," he stammered. "He is a welcome help to our journey." He looked again at Trecia, who cast her eyes down while her face pinked. "And you are?"

Phoebe stood, then wiped the remnants of fig and bread from her mouth. "I am Phoebe."

"Phoebe. A nice name, that." But his eyes stayed upon Trecia. "And you are?"

Trecia stood, smiling. "Trecia. I am accompanying Phoebe on a mission."

Phoebe elbowed Trecia, but the girl would not capitulate. "We are bringing something important to Rome."

"Would you excuse us?" Phoebe asked.

"Of course. But I came to introduce myself. I am Longinus."

Phoebe wanted to say, "For such a short man, your name is irony," but she held her tongue.

Trecia smiled and met his gaze. "It is my pleasure to make your acquaintance."

Longinus bowed before them, his right hand behind him. "The joy is all mine, I assure you. A journey like this can be full of dangers, and you will need an ally." He kept his gaze upon Trecia, and she did not break free from it until Phoebe pulled her away.

"A word," she said.

With that, Longinus put up his hands as if in surrender and walked away, taking his place among the rigging.

Phoebe turned to Trecia. "What do you mean by telling him of our mission?" She took Trecia's elbow, directing her to the ship's railing where the wind would providentially steal their voices.

"You never told me *not* to." Trecia's voice sounded small as the breeze picked up.

"Its secrecy was implied."

"But not spoken." Trecia's gaze shifted toward Longinus, who returned the favor.

"He is not a part of our quest, and he could become our undoing." Although the sun warmed most of her, she could not get her hands warm. She wrung them out of habit from a life-long bout with cold extremities. Even her toes stayed cold in a warm communal bath.

"He is harmless. You forget that God sometimes sends helpers and allies. How do you know he is a foe? Why do you jump to such conclusions?"

Phoebe kept silent. Perhaps Trecia spoke truth. Her default was to jump to the worst in people, something Paul had warned about when he spoke in the Corinthian church. Love was to be vulnerable like that—to believe all things, hope all things, endure all things. It should never assume the worst, but hope for the best. "I am sorry," she said finally. She thought of his short stature. "He does look harmless."

Trecia grabbed Phoebe's hands in hers, accustomed to their unspoken ritual. She rubbed her warm hands together over Phoebe's cold fingers. "Your poor hands," she said.

Trecia sang a hymn familiar to them both as the friction of warm hands to cold hands brought life back to Phoebe. It was as if the simple action renewed her vigor and reminded her afresh that God loved her. He would take care of them all. And His plan would prevail. "Thank you. I am sorry for the accusa-tion. But please hear me. We must be careful. This is precious cargo we carry." She pointed to the satchel that hung across her body. The scrolls were treasure, and they deserved to live next to her heart. Now if only she could finally believe the same about herself. After the death of Albus, she asked the questions: Was she treasured? Did God dare to live next to her heart? Could He be trusted when the world slipped away? When she lost everything familiar? When her husband's body was lowered into the gaping earth? Was God good then? She worked her way through those questions, but like pesky mosquitoes, they'd emerge during times of distress. Was He good now? Could He be trusted? Oh how she wanted to fully believe those words.

"I am young," Trecia said this with determination, it seemed to Phoebe—a declaration of sorts. "And I know I have a limited life."

Phoebe tasted fear at those words. "Are you not well?"

Trecia laughed. "No, I am well. It is simply a statement of fact. I know I am a servant, and I will never have an opportunity like this again—to see the world, to sail beneath the sun, to step foot on the cobbles of Rome. If I forget my manners by talking to a crewmember or laughing too loud or making a mistake in etiquette, I hope you can forgive me. This may be the only adventure of my life. I intend to soak it in as we bathe beneath the sun's rays. It is delicious to me." She smiled more broadly than Phoebe had ever seen, as if her smile drank in joy.

"You know that I see you more than merely a servant—you are my sister in Christ."

"Yes, of course. We are companions, those who break bread together, who worship the same God, who bear burdens and share prayers. But our stature is ranked differently. I am more like Joses, though he be freed, than you. I am more like him." She pointed to Longinus.

"You are clothed with dignity."

Trecia sighed. "I have made my peace with my position in rank. How else are any of us supposed to live except to accept our lot in life and find joy in the margins? And I intend to do just that. Isn't that what your friend Paul says?"

Phoebe looked beneath them at the seas churning below. She did not know how to swim, so this ship held her captive. "Paul is your friend too, is he not?"

Trecia nodded. "He is always speaking of rejoicing, is he not?"

The waves continued their monotonous dance, splashing relentlessly on the vessel's sides. These same waves had seen the unfolding of history, she knew. They existed before her first breath, before Jesus's conception, before the prophets Paul quoted, before the sin of King David, before the patriarchs. The world God created continued its ceaseless being, seemingly unaffected by humanity's demise. *We live. We die.* Rejoicing was one of the doctrines Paul preached that Phoebe dismissed as trivial. "But life—it is serious. It is dire. We must do our duty."

"But cannot duty be a joyful one? Why not laugh at the days to come? Why not relish the moment? Why not smile sometimes at good fortune?" Trecia nearly sang the words. They seemed to float from her mouth, joining the seas in an undulating hum of praise.

Phoebe pulled in a salt-aired breath. Having lived in Corinth all her life, she grew accustomed to the scent of seawater, but here she could taste it on her tongue. The lingering sweetness of the figs gave way to salt's tang. Hadn't Jesus spoken of such things? That all who followed Him were salt, just as He was salt? A preservative? A much needed seasoning? Something utterly different among the blandness? Perhaps akin to joy? "Yes," she finally said. "You are right. I must remember joy, though I admit it is not my bent."

Trecia laughed at her words. "Perhaps you will find joy in me." She took Phoebe's right hand in her left, then squeezed it. "You can be assured of my continual presence, and, hopefully, that will keep your heart at rest."

The sun, once brilliant, now hid behind a dark gray cloud, causing Phoebe to shiver. How could the weather turn so quickly? The wind whipped the sail into a frenzy above them, while the sky darkened. Rain spat from the sky.

Joses returned to the two of them, his eyes full of concern. "Best go beneath the deck," he told them. "The weather has shifted."

Phoebe remembered the small room they would call their home for over a week, the stench that emanated from it, the tenor of her stomach. "We can stay above. It is only rain."

"No, it is more than rain. Rain is benign. It is the stirring of the seas we must concern ourselves with. Please heed my advice, Phoebe, Trecia." He looked at them both. "And find safety beneath."

Joses placed strong hands on both of their elbows, guiding them toward the portal below. He held Phoebe's right hand as she descended, then Trecia's. Trecia disappeared into their little room, but Phoebe looked up through the opening toward the sky beyond Joses's head. The clouds churned as if they were engaged in an angry fight, throwing pots of water into the opening. She tried to brush away the onslaught, but the water continued to bathe her. "You should join us," she yelled to the opening, not entirely sure if Joses still stood there.

"My duty is to keep this boat afloat and you, Trecia, and the cargo safe. But I would appreciate one thing," he yelled.

"What is that?"

"Prayers."

And with that, the hatch slammed shut, reverberating through the ship. The vessel creaked and moaned as it rocked to and fro, back and forth—seemingly all motions at once. They were riders upon an untrained, angry horse who galloped and bucked and reared in hopes of loosing itself of them. Phoebe held her stomach, joined Trecia in the awful room, and said her prayers.

CHAPTER TEN

The last time Phoebe begged for death, it was at the behest of her grief. Albus's death had not been a simple one, nor had it been swift. He lay upon a bed-turned-dais in their home, his lips blue, his chest wracked with fits of coughing. His was a labored air, so much so that she found herself straining to breathe, willing her exhale into his inhale. Many times as Phoebe sat by his side, she caught herself holding her breath as his held. *Breathe,* she told herself. "Breathe," she encouraged him.

The blood had quivered through her insides then too. Albus, always an achiever in his own right, overachieved when he coughed. Initially it had been spittle, clear and easy. But more erupted, producing differing colors of green and brown sputum, eventually tingeing with blood. And once the tinge occurred, it roared into heartbreaking reality. She lost count of how many times she put a cloth to her husband's mouth, only to pull it back, bloodied. And with every new cloth came new revelations of red. "God in heaven," she heard herself pray then. "Take me instead. Wreck me instead. Heal my husband!" But those cries and prayers and whispers and moans turned into groanings too deep for words, and Albus slowly succumbed to his illness, a desperate fading that willed to steal her resolve.

He who had been healed of so much now battled pestilence.

"Phoebe, please do not—"

She placed her fingers upon his lips. "Shush. I know it hurts to talk."

Trecia scurried around them, heating water, opening and then closing draperies to let in the good air, expel the bad. But no matter how Phoebe worked and fevered her preparations, no matter how she dutifully obeyed the physician's orders, Albus continued his decline. But in this holy place of degradation, Phoebe suddenly became aware of Trecia's presence and dubbed it an annoyance instead of aid. "May we have a moment alone?" Her voice, she knew, hinted at irritation, but Trecia did not respond; she simply faded from view. The girl understood, Phoebe knew.

"Albus," she whispered to her husband. "What is it? Do you need more covering? Less? Warmth? Cool air?" She hoped he could communicate his needs without speech because every word was spent as if from a bank—when it left his lips, it was gone forever, along with another level of energy.

He struggled to sit up.

"No, lie back down."

But he would not. Instead he righted himself, pulled in a ragged breath, and looked at Phoebe with longing. "You are beautiful."

Tears left her eyes then. She wished she had a way of capturing those three words for eternity, placing them in an alabaster vial to be heard at any moment of the day once uncorked. But they were gone, though he still breathed.

A mournful dove sang a song to its lover outside the window, the familiar three-toned melody. It seemed to say, "He is leaving, leaving, leaving."

"I love you," she told her husband. "You are my light, my song."

"Only Jesus," he said. "He alone."

She knew his meaning—as those who had been married any length of time had decoded each other's moods and words, understanding their subtext. He wanted her to be cautious of idolatry, of placing him as supreme importance over their Savior. Jesus, he was communicating, meant everything and should hold the highest of her affections and allegiance. "Of course, darling. Jesus will be with me forever. He is everything to me. But you have been Him to me—a tangible representation of His affection. I cannot get over that. Nor do I ever want to. It was you who demonstrated for me the wisdom of the Way. You who modeled prayer. You who shared my heart with the God who sees. You whose hands produced miracles in the name of Jesus. We have seen so much, have we not?"

Albus nodded.

"I will trust no other," she said.

"No." Albus coughed, then spat more blood. His face turned blue.

She patted him on the back with force, hoping to dislodge what had fastened like eagle talons to his lungs, his throat, his will.

He fell back down upon his bed. "Please. For me. Live your life. You must live."

She held his face in her hands, feeling the heat of the fever that consumed him. She smoothed the sweat from his prominent brow, wondering if his family knew the gravity of his situation. When she and Albus had abandoned all to follow the narrow road of Jesus, both of their families turned from confidants to combatants. Would his parents stand above his gravesite? Would they sing their pagan funeral songs? Would they mourn? Or was it that they had mourned already when they made the decision to disown? As Albus struggled with breath, Phoebe wrestled with anger. With his parents. With hers. With their state of aloneness, save the church. She felt untethered then, floating above the earth without anchor, like a sail cut free from its moorings and let to fly heavenward. Would she ever find home once Albus succumbed? Oh, they had prayed. Paul had laid rough, tent-making hands upon Albus, but this time the Almighty's will was suffering, not solace. Others prayed, believing, then walked away, leaving her to her grief. It was one thing to be disowned by one's family and grieve that death. It was quite another to watch the life empty slowly from one you loved so fiercely.

Albus opened his moistened eyes. His eyelashes fluttered, so long, so delicate, so beautiful, she thought. His face contorted in the afternoon light while the doves called back and forth to each other. "I must tell you something," he said.

She bent closer. "Whisper. It will save your strength." She told herself to steady her voice, fearing if tears erupted, Albus would finally understand the gravity of his situation and give up.

"I want…you…to…" He coughed convulsively, spat hemorrhages into the cloth he clutched at his mouth.

She grabbed it, threw it to the floor, and quickly replaced it with a clean one. "Save your voice. Please."

"Serve," he said, "the church. They need you. But—"

"We will do that together, as we always have." She pushed away an errant hair, realizing she perspired as well.

"I will see you on the other—"

"No! Please do not speak that way, dear Albus. We serve a God who heals. Nothing is too difficult for Him. Sickness must flee at His name. Jesus. Jesus. Jesus. Please heal my husband." She collapsed upon him, the two seeming to be one flesh in that moment. She felt the blessed rise of his chest, the beating of his heart beating a beautiful rhythm into her ears. She willed him to live. Prayed that he would. Begged God for mercy.

Albus, with much effort, pulled his hand from his side and placed his arm over her while she wept. The afternoon faded to dusk while the doves cried and his heartbeat slowed, seeming to skip every fourth beat. His breathing faded to shallow gasps.

"No, my dear. No. Do not leave me."

"I have loved you well," he rasped. "But please be aware of one thing."

"What is it?"

"Obey. Obey Jesus, no matter what. Nothing else matters," he said.

At this, Trecia entered the room. "Is there anything I can bring? Anything at all?"

"Can you not see he is dying? Please leave us alone!" Phoebe's forceful words surprised even her, and Trecia obeyed, slinking into the corridor.

She turned to face Albus, to gaze into his clear eyes that continued to tear up. As long as tears moistened his eyes, he was alive, and she was determined to be utterly present in the moment. Her mind wandered to the many miracles she had seen in the Corinthian church over the years. Eyesight restored. Withered hands straightened. Bleeding stopped. The same God lived in the midst of them both, so she prayed again. "Lord Jesus, Son of God, healer of the nations, hear my prayer. Please have mercy upon me, a sinner. Have mercy upon Albus. He is Your servant. He loves You. There is much work for him to do for Your kingdom. Please do not take him from this earth. Please do not leave me alone, without my husband. I am too weak. My strength is small. My heart is wearied. I cannot endure widowhood. I cannot endure this life. Please heal him."

But no matter how she pled, no matter how many prayers she threw heavenward, the words seemed to stop at her ceiling, bouncing back upon her while Albus siphoned in breath.

"I see!" He sat up suddenly, eyes wide. "You are here!"

Phoebe's eyes followed Albus's gaze that rested on the window where the doves continued their plaintive cries.

"Oh, the light!"

In this moment, Albus became transformed. His eyes brightened. His breathing remeasured itself into normalcy. His cheeks regained their color. "I will tell her!" With this he looked once again at Phoebe, though she could see what he really wanted to do was to talk to the window. "You must be careful. Do not let betrayal steal your resolve. Rest in the love of God which is in Christ Jesus, dear one." With that, he turned toward the window, then tried to struggle to his feet.

Phoebe tried to get him to sit back down, but he would not. He stood, wavering, arms outstretched toward the window. "I am undone and done. Yes. Yes. I am healed!"

In that moment a rush of wind blew through the window, swirling around them both. *Yes*, Phoebe thought, *this is what our miracle will look like. He is being healed!* As a tree toppled to the forest floor, however, Albus fell back upon his bed, an open-mouthed smile teasing his lips as he exhaled his final breath. When he hit his pillow, life left his body.

Never to return.

Phoebe heard her voice weeping, from deep within her chest, but she felt as if she were not in the room, not experiencing such shock.

Trecia returned, eyes wide. "I heard the commotion," she said. She looked upon Albus, who lay still as death. "Oh no. Oh my dear Phoebe, no." She pulled Phoebe to her, stroked her hair, and sang a hymn of consolation as she wept.

But all Phoebe wanted was the voice and breath of her dear Albus, not Trecia's presence. How would she continue on? Breaking away from her friend's kindhearted embrace, she knelt beside Albus, touched his cooling hand, unruffled his hair, then closed his eyes with her fingertips. He was dead.

"Fetch my sackcloth," she heard herself say. "Alert the mourners. It is time for grief to make its home here."

Trecia left while Phoebe sat still as night. Albus returned no affection, said no words. Suddenly she felt completely abandoned, as if the universe had de-peopled itself of all save her. As tears ran down her cheeks, the mourning doves ceased their singing. Silence.

It was then she begged God to steal her breath, to seal her in heaven with Albus. But He did not oblige her request.

And while the ship beneath her bucked and hiccupped upon the water as she clutched her stomach and Trecia retched, she prayed the same prayer of deliverance—except not to be delivered to death but to be deposited to Rome, scrolls in hand.

But as Trecia clung to her in the dank hovel they called home, as waves beat strong against the boat's hull, as she prayed for a shard of hope in light of her waning strength, the persistent knock of Joses above kept her from giving in to fear's grasp.

Knock. Knock. Knock.

CHAPTER ELEVEN

The relentless onslaught of water, waves, and rain pelted the ship for hours upon hours. It was hard for Phoebe to discern between dawn, midday, and dusk, but when the darkness fell, it came suddenly like ink spilled upon scroll. She could not see her hand in front of her. She willed herself to sleep, and eventually, her lids grew heavy, and she entered the land of dreams.

A sudden crack awakened her—it sounded like the ship itself broke in half, but she could not be sure if it was her imagination or the reality of their voyage.

She instinctively called out for Trecia then but received no answer. Phoebe blindly searched along the wooden walls of their bunker, but her fingers did not alight on Trecia. *Where is she?*

Soggy to the bone, she crept from the room, calling out for Trecia, but the roar of the wind above swallowed her voice. "Trecia!" She felt her way toward the ladder, then pulled her way upward, pushing with everything inside her upon the secured hatch. It wouldn't budge. She tried again, to no avail. Desperate, she returned to their room, calling for Trecia again. It was then she heard the comforting triple knock of Joses above. Phoebe strained on her toes toward the ceiling and returned the knock, then yelled. "Joses!"

Faintly, she could hear the timbre of his voice. "What is it? Are you hurt?"

"No! I cannot find Trecia. I need your help. Open the hatch," she yelled.

"I will be right there."

Within minutes, he stood at the threshold of her doorway, waterlogged, dripping. "Do you have a torch?"

"No."

"I will seek one."

Joses came back with a torch, its warmth illuminating his face. He tripped sideways as the boat rolled starboard, then righted himself. "Are you sure you want to come with me? It is a dangerous wind."

"She is my responsibility. I must go."

Joses offered his wet hand her way. "For safety," he said.

She took it, and they tripped their way through the bowels of the vessel. Up ahead she saw a crooked doorway with a sliver of light breaking through. "There," she shouted.

Joses pressed on toward the doorway, holding Phoebe's hand—not too firmly, thankfully. He pushed it open, exposing a group of sailors laughing, drinking, singing, seemingly to the boat's rocking. Longinus stood. Nodded at Joses. "Sir, is there a problem?"

"We are seeking Trecia, Phoebe's servant. Have you seen her?"

It was precisely at this time that Longinus stepped aside, revealing Trecia standing behind him, a sheepish look upon her face. With her hair exposed and in ringlets, no palla covering the mane, Phoebe once again saw the young maiden's beauty, but also her naivete. "You scared me." She passed through the crowd of foul-smelling men to reach her.

"You were asleep," she said. "And I was scared."

"We will speak of this later. Now come."

Trecia sighed and then looked at Longinus. "Thank you for protecting me." Trecia flashed a look of anger Phoebe's way—something that both unnerved and startled her. Was *she* not Trecia's protector? Trecia's allegiance must first be to Christ and their task, yet she willingly chose to abandon Phoebe to the dank closet. She tried to gather her thoughts as Joses led them by torch away from the belly of the boat toward their mutual prison.

They smelled their quarters first.

"I am sorry you have to endure such hardships," Joses said. "If I could I would take the stench upon me for your sakes. I have worked in worse conditions my entire life." He shoved the torch into their little chamber. "Ah! Perhaps this accounts for the odor." He brought the torch to the back left corner where a pile of carcasses lay. "Rats," he said. "Do you have any extra cloths I can have, by chance?"

Phoebe stifled her angst, which normally would have resulted in a scream. Vermin were her weakness—even Trecia knew such a thing. She told herself not to startle and fixed her focus on the request at hand. She retrieved a woolen stola and handed it to Joses.

"Here, hold the torch." While Phoebe held it steady, the boat continued its maniacal rocking. She had to brace both feet to keep herself upright. Trecia retreated to the other corner, saying nothing.

Joses gathered the dead rats into the garment, then motioned for Phoebe to shine the light in every nook and cranny of the room. He pointed out a few more, one of which twitched under the gaze of the light.

At this Phoebe did scream. Thankfully, the creaking of the boat added to the symphony. Scream. Creak. Scream. Creak.

Joses collected all the decay. "I will dispose of them over the side," he said.

Phoebe sighed in relief. "Do you need me to follow with the torch?"

"No," he said. "This is a task I can do in the dark. In the meantime, stay close, keep the torch, and try to dry out as much as you can."

"We will." Phoebe held the torch steady in the middle of the tiny room.

"And take mind of your feet. They don't do well when water-logged." This was Joses's last piece of advice before he disappeared upward into the night, taking the stench with him.

Phoebe could now see Trecia's face. She could not tell whether it was wet from precipitation or tears. "Why did you leave me?" She wanted to say, *I trusted you,* but decided to believe the best of her young friend. Better to hear someone out than barge forward with untested accusations.

"I told you," Trecia said, this time her voice softened. "I was entirely afraid. And when Longinus knocked to check in on us, you were sound asleep. He seemed to know my fright and invited me to the ship's center where the back-and-forth was less. I am sorry. I should not have left you, dear Phoebe. Can you ever forgive me?"

By now, Phoebe had found a gap in the floor of their little quarters and had wedged the torch within it. Soon she would blow it out, knowing that too much torch smoke in an enclosed space would harm them both, but for now she needed to see the contours of her longtime companion's face. "I follow Jesus Christ, who said, 'Father, forgive them, for they do not know what they are doing' from the cross. So of course I want to be a woman of forgiveness. But I must admit I was shocked at your behavior. It was you amidst a group of men. Not only did that put you in danger, as you can imagine, but it also gave the appearance of evil. What would others think? Would they jump to the conclusion that you were a harlot?"

Trecia laughed. Her wet hair continued to curl in on itself. "I am hardly harlot material."

"It matters what others think of your character. You have to see that."

"But God looks at the heart, not at outward appearance—as in the case of King David. You are the one who told me that story. So why are you putting a new standard upon me? That is what Paul preached against, was it not? That we would not add to the Gospel rules that had nothing to do with them?"

"But he also spoke of chastity, of living above suspicion, and conducting ourselves in a manner worthy of the Gospel of God."

Trecia shook her head. "And what are you implying?"

"Nothing. Nothing at all. It simply appeared—"

"Appearances can be deceiving. Nevertheless, I cannot convince you of my innocence. You will have to trust that my utmost allegiance is to you and your safety. I was a little out of sorts when the boat creaked under the storm, and for that I am very sorry. I let my fear dictate my actions, and you paid the price. I have really spoken too much in my defense. My job is simply to love you."

"I hope it is not a painful occupation." Phoebe folded her hands upon her lap, remembering how Albus used the comment favorably.

Trecia reached out, placed both hands on hers. "It is my joy. Please forgive me."

"Of course," Phoebe said. She may be widowed, forsaken of her family, but God had not left her abandoned. She had Trecia—young and naive, yes, but faithful. She had the kindness of Joses, though something niggled her about him. She had the goodness of God, who kept them alive in the midst of the storm. She had the scrolls held to her body with leather, which would bring hope to the burgeoning group of believers in Rome. And she had hope. Always, hope. It was what the Israelites lost sight of, allowing fear to overtake them in the wilderness. It was the same fear the disciples displayed when they disbelieved Jesus's provision after He fed five thousand with loaves and fishes and another crowd faced them. *How quickly we all doubt,* she reminded herself. *How quickly we focus on the panic at hand rather than the Lord's provision.* How swift her feet were to run to worry.

"Let us sing away the storm," Trecia said.

Phoebe nodded. "I need to blow this out first." She tried several times to extinguish the burning stick with her breath, but it simply would not obey. Finally she remembered where they were, how doused the small room was, and she plunged the head of the torch into a puddle formed to her left. The torch sizzled out.

They sang, voices lilting above the cacophony of the storm, and as they harmonized, the storm seemed to obey their voices. Slowly, almost imperceptibly, it diminished. The rocking turned to a gentle sway. The rain transformed from torrent to trickle. The thunder went to sleep, stopped its roaring.

Perhaps everything will be fine, Phoebe thought.

"I almost forgot!"

Trecia's sudden outburst startled Phoebe. "Is everything all right?"

"More so! As I packed for our voyage, at the last moment, I threw in something that would save us, but it was such a last-minute addition, I completely forgot about it."

"What is it?"

Trecia fumbled through her small satchel and sighed. "This!"

"You remember I cannot see in the dark."

Trecia placed something beneath her nose. Phoebe inhaled and then smiled. Lavender. Blessed lavender.

"This room will smell of home," she said. She handed Phoebe a long stalk of the flower. Phoebe knew just what to do. She rolled the dried flower between her palms, releasing the heady scent into the confines of their room.

Their song had ascended like a pleasing aroma to the throne room of God, and now the flowers mimicked their worship. "Thank you," Phoebe said, "for remembering such a small thing."

"I have found that the smallest of things carry the greatest of treasures." Trecia's voice sounded weary, and soon she stopped speaking altogether and succumbed to the rhythms of sleep.

Apt words, Phoebe thought. She touched the leather satchel that had become her second skin. She certainly felt small compared to the task of delivering God's words to a body of believers. The worry of it all still loomed large in her mind. But Trecia's simple words, coupled with the tiny grains of lavender that scented an entire space, reminded her of the power of small. A tiny mustard seed grew to provide shade. A shepherd became a giant killer. A simple Carpenter became a King. Perhaps it would be that a widow became a messenger. Little was much in the hands of the One who created it all.

The sea no longer frightened her tonight, though she had to admit that once its rage died down, it was easy for her to assert such confidence. Tomorrow would take care of itself— no need to borrow trouble tonight. As sleep wooed her, she kept the praise of God upon her lips while she clutched the satchel to her chest.

CHAPTER TWELVE

With dawn came joy, reminding Phoebe of the beautiful words, *weeping may last for a night, but joy comes in the morning.* Light pierced through the planks above, welcoming her to the day.

She took note of Trecia sound asleep next to her, then smoothed the woolen stola over her shoulders. She lightly touched it, wondering if this was what mothers did with their daughters—even when they reached womanhood. The familiar pang of childlessness hit her in the womb, and she mourned again. There would be no child to carry on the name of Albus or to reveal her heart to the next generation. Theirs was an interrupted love story that would stop at this generation. Perhaps this voyage would be her last exclamation, the message she would convey to the world. Although she was not prone to pride in quite that way—longing for fame or a name for herself—she did long for legacy, that how she conducted her life since meeting Christ would somehow make an advancement of the kingdom of God, however small.

While Trecia's eyes flickered dreams unaware, Phoebe stood. She pulled off the satchel and opened it like a mouth. Inside rested the two scrolls, safe and dry. She pulled each out, caressing the soft papyrus, feeling the raised edge of each seal.

These would be her children, her legacy. She slipped them safely back, pulled the satchel over her shoulders, and left the faintly lavender-scented room.

The ladder now opened to the sky, the hatch having been pushed open by some unseen force—or had it been by the hand of Joses? She pulled herself up the ladder, rung over rung and blinked into the daylight. The brilliance of the sun nearly stung her eyes, but with all the gloom and wet from the previous day, she made her peace with it by laughing.

"It is a beautiful day," she heard Joses say to her left.

"Indeed."

"I have a moment between shifts of labor. Enjoy the morning with me?" He patted the coil of ropes next to him. "It's hardly a seat for a lady, but it is what I have, so I offer it to you freely."

Phoebe sat next to him there while the sun frolicked upon the water, and the sail flapped in a capricious wind—if you could call it such.

"This will be a long day with short distance, I am afraid." He pointed to the distant shoreline behind them. "We made no progress in the storm. My hunch is that it forced us to lose what we had gained."

Phoebe sighed. "So not a ten-day voyage, then?"

He shook his head, stroking his beard. "I am afraid not. But at least the day brings sun and warmth."

They sat there a moment while Phoebe collected her thoughts. There had been something in Joses's way that intrigued yet bothered her. He had not seemed to shed his penchant for servitude. "So you were a slave," she said finally.

Joses inhaled, then let out a long breath. "It is as you say."

"I am not quite familiar with that life."

"I am quite familiar with it," he said.

A fish jumped to their left and then plunged seaward. A crying gull dove to the surface, grabbing the flapping fish in its bill, then flew away. "Yours was a short servitude?"

"I wish it was." He said nothing for a long time while a series of gulls raided the sea of fish, and the sun grew warmer by the moment.

She watched the birds soar above them, hoping they would not defecate upon them. "But you are free," she said.

"It is a long story."

"I have a long time. More than ten days, apparently."

Joses bent forward, head in hands. He rubbed his face and then put his hands upon his knees. He looked at Phoebe. "How familiar are you with the history of Israel?"

"Fairly. The apostle Paul had much to say about his history, though he counted his time as a Pharisee as rubbish in order to gain the knowledge of Jesus Christ."

"The rhythm of Sabbath was to be the rhythm of indentured servitude. Six years a slave, then released the seventh. And then the year of Jubilee was supposed to dawn after seven sevens. But the spirit of the law was that no Jewish person would be enslaved beyond those six years. However, if he loved where he worked and longed to be dedicated to his master's family, he could pierce his ear with an awl and become a bondservant." Joses turned toward her, a pained look upon his face. He pointed to his ear. A hole graced it.

"So you were a bondservant."

"I have heard others say it is a beautiful representation of how the believer is related to his Savior, but for me, it was forced—something I did not choose. In the middle of the night, as I lay asleep, the owner of the estate I worked coerced a few men to pin me to my bed. They forced my ear upon an earthen brick, and pierced it without my assent."

"I cannot imagine such barbarian practices."

"It is the world we live in, Phoebe. One you know so little about. Paul told me that Jesus said the poor you always have with you. Oh, but their voices are quiet."

She wanted to apologize but stayed silent. His words were not laced with blame or condemnation, just brokenness.

"The entire situation reminded me of a terrible time in Israel's history, when we were about to be besieged by Nebuchadnezzar of Babylon. King Zedekiah, as the city was being ransacked, made a covenant with the people that all the slaves should be set free. No one was to keep a fellow country-man in bondage. The people of Israel readily agreed—for a time. But eventually they took back every slave, male and female alike."

"Why?"

"I suppose it was fear, but nonetheless, it happened," Joses said. "Injustice reigns when man fears for his livelihood. Or in the case of Joseph, vengeance is the impetus."

"At the hand of his brothers," she said.

"His story informs mine, particularly as I try to love Jesus. So much of Joseph's life paralleled Jesus's. Both forsaken. Both suffering unjustly. Both wrongly accused. It has been the model of Joseph that has become my song."

"In what ways?"

"When Joseph finally confronted those who sold him to slavery, his very own flesh and blood, he chose grace over justice. He said, 'You intended to harm me, but God intended it for good to accomplish what is now being done, the saving of many lives.' God used his slavery to bring him on a journey of deliverance. Though it has not always been easy for me to understand this, I am coming to see that God has used my own servitude to bring me to this exact place, where I can be part of a new mission—to bring words of life to those who need it. Yes, harm happened. But good is coming too. This is the way of God—to deliver us so we can be part of delivering messages to others. It's not my task to punish those I perceive to be villains. As Christ's ambassador, I choose to look forward to those He wants me to help."

"I commend you for such a viewpoint," she said.

Joses sat again beside her. "This is the heart of the Gospel we love. We turn from bondage to sin, to freedom in grace. That is what our friend Paul often preaches."

"Do you think the apostle has long on this earth?"

Joses shook his head. "He is as bold as a lion, though sickness often overtakes him. The Spirit of God is strong within him, which makes him an enemy of the forces of darkness. I have no doubt there are dubious plans against his life."

Phoebe had been worrying about this very thing. She heard rumors of prophecies that Paul would one day be in Jerusalem, then Rome as well, but that he would not leave alive. This saddened her, but as she remembered the last breaths of dear Albus, she was all too familiar with the brevity of life and humanity's short sojourn upon the earth. "I wonder why, when Jesus conquered death for us all, we still have to endure it?"

"There are many mysteries to be solved upon this earth." He pointed to the water. "And upon this sea. But I do not pretend to understand them. We are simply tasked with bending the knee before the One who created it all, worshipping Him alone, and heeding the Spirit's call within us. So many times, God reminded the nation of Israel that to obey Him was far better than a superficial sacrifice. And I have found obedience, at times, to be excruciating. Is this how you see it as well?"

"Yes." She pointed to herself, where the satchel lay across her ribcage. "I worry much about whether we will find success in our journey. I know the gravity of Paul's request, the importance of these documents. Though I am weak, I consider myself blessed of God to be given such a task. I am humbled by it all. But I am also scared."

Joses did not take her hand as Albus would do when she admitted fear before him. He simply sat beside her and nodded. Could a man such as this be truly afraid? Had he not seen atrocities and labors that would break a man in two? Why would this journey bring fear to a man so strong? She left these questions to roll around like rocks on an incline on the soil of her mind. Perhaps she was braver than she thought. No. Maybe all of humanity struggled with clay-footed insecurity.

A gull deposited its excrement at her feet. She pulled them back and exclaimed.

Joses laughed, full hearted. His beard shook in the effort.

"Funny for you, but it nearly hit me," Phoebe said.

"Near misses are humorous, do you think?"

She followed the pathway of the gull across the impossibly azure sky. It flew freely, unhindered—as free as Joses's laugh. She felt his story in her heart, empathizing with his plight, the forced piercing, the untold story that came out in his body language but not his tongue. "I am sorry for your story," she said.

He stood, offering his hand. He lifted her to her feet, an easy effort. "Do not be sorry for a story God continues to write. There is redemption yet—at least, that is my hope." He pointed to her satchel, smiling. "I am grateful I get to be a part of this voyage."

She nearly said thank you, but something inside held the words inside. Instead she said, "I must go wake Trecia."

CHAPTER THIRTEEN

When Phoebe returned to their small bunk, Trecia was not there. From the ship's belly she heard shouting and the stomping of feet. Phoebe swallowed and took a measured breath. She made her way toward the commotion. "What is happening?" she yelled to the darkness, worrying that perhaps her voice had been too forceful. She knew her place in the order of the lives of men, but her fear made her forget her propriety.

A hand gently held hers. "I am here," Trecia whispered—her voice a seeming warning to Phoebe to keep hers in check.

"Why were you not in our room?" Phoebe whispered back.

"Let us go atop the boat," Trecia said. "I have some news of import."

So for the second time that day, Phoebe squinted into the sunlight. In the meantime, Joses had returned to his labors, his back sweating beneath the relentless heat. She motioned for Trecia to join her there. "What was happening? Are you all right?"

"All is well. You worry far too much." She pointed to the gulls circling the sky in lazy circles. "Remember what Jesus told His disciples about birds—that they do not have to worry about what to eat because God provides for them, that lilies do not have to spin fabric to clothe themselves with beauty, that worrying is borrowing tomorrow's trouble."

Phoebe laughed. "Yes, Paul has told me as much. He has spent much time with those who walked roads of Israel with Jesus. There are many stories like this—Jesus calming a raging sea, feeding thousands with one small meal, delivering the demoniac from the clutches of the devil, healing a man blind from birth. There are times, though, like today, when I wish He was sitting right beside me, comforting me when I fret."

Trecia shielded her eyes from the sun with her hand. "You are the one who has told me we are never alone, never without God. The Spirit lives within you, right? And as a dove descended upon Jesus, so the Spirit infiltrates the hearts of those who believe. You are not forsaken. You are never chased away."

"Yes, it is as you say." Phoebe put her hand to her chest, wondering afresh if such a mystery was true. Yes, she had felt the transformation the moment she believed, and the Spirit within her certainly gave her the fortitude she needed to stay true to the Messiah when her family shunned and scorned her. But today? In the chaos of the rabble-rousing of men at sea? When her mission felt precarious and slowed to a turtle's pace? Was He with her? Would He continue to deliver her? She knew there were no guarantees once the Spirit of God rested upon and within her, that it would be the normal call to be persecuted and harmed. So why did she give way to fear now? Especially in the light of day when the air smelled of promise?

Trecia pulled her close. She could feel the younger woman's breath upon her cheek. "There is talk of danger," she said.

"Is that why everyone was yelling and stomping just now?"

"Yes. A rumor had surfaced, and Captain Regulus was trying to calm the fears of the men, which is why I left our little room—the commotion it created."

"What was said?"

"There is talk of sea raiders," she whispered.

Phoebe looked to the sky. What now? Storms, she had weathered. Persecution? Yes. But sea raiders? "What do you mean?"

"These waters are teeming with them, apparently. It is considered an actual occupation by some, just as thieves consider it their job to relieve the rich of their resources. Instead of creating industry and shipping goods, they simply take what has already been paid for by overtaking a crew and ship, then receiving the pilfered payment when they deliver the payload." Trecia stood, then pointed toward the east at the rear of the boat. "See there?"

Phoebe strained to see a few specks on the eastern horizon. "Just barely."

"Those could be sea raiders. Or not. Captain Regulus has assured me that they are not, but Longinus does not believe his confident words. He tells such frightening stories, Phoebe."

Phoebe shook her head. "You must be careful with Longinus. I believe he finds you beautiful, and when a man bewitches himself with a woman, he will do anything to attract her attention. He will tell stories. He will instill fear so she will perhaps reach for his hand."

Trecia laughed, then turned away. She leaned against the railing, bending at the waist while the wind pulled at tendrils of her hair, once kept up, now frenzied. "It is not as you think, dear Phoebe. He is more like a brother to me than one interested in marriage."

"I am not convinced. Please assure me that you will be cautious."

"Do you want to know of the rumors or not?"

Joses returned from rigging and dipped a ladle into a large barrel for a drink of water. "What rumors?" he asked.

"Sea raiding," Phoebe said. "Have you heard about it?"

He leaned backward a body length from Trecia, only he faced her, not the waves. "Yes, of course. This is a known truth. Did not Paul warn you of such dangers?"

Phoebe tried to retrace her conversations with Paul, but she could not remember stories of sea raiding. The only warning had come from Joses. She shook her head.

"I am sorry he did not. Perhaps he thought this would be a truth universally known. This sea is a tumultuous one, but the tumult comes not merely from waves and storms, but humanity bent on taking. Yes, Phoebe, there are sea raiders. And we must be diligent. This is why I was tasked to protect you, Trecia, and the treasure you carry."

Trecia turned so they both faced her now. "What would we do if sea raiders overtook the ship?"

Joses cleared his throat. "There is not much to do, but to playact indifference, go about our lives, and not bring attention to ourselves or our mission. Most likely a sea raider will only be interested in taking the cargo to port—in order to be recompensed for the stolen goods. He and his crew will not concern themselves with passengers traveling on holiday—which is the story we will tell."

"This is no holiday," Phoebe said. And all the worry she began the day with rose from her gut into her mind, afflicting her head. She pressed her thumbs to her temples, trying to stem the tide of pain. It did not work.

"Oh, I see," Trecia said. "We tell a common story. What exactly should we say—what are the details we must keep consistent among us?" Her voice sounded to Phoebe a bit too singsong, as if this were a game, and the danger was simply a paltry possibility to be played along with.

Joses dipped another ladle into the nearby barrel and pulled in another drink, returning to lean against the railing near Trecia. "I will not be a part of the story, for your protection, but I will do everything I can to keep you both safe."

"Why will you not be part?" Phoebe asked.

"If I am here to offer protection, then the sea raiders will want to know what I am protecting."

"Is it not enough to say you are protecting two women on a voyage?" Phoebe wondered at his logic.

"I can blend into the crew," he said. "But if I am connected with you, they will ask more questions than necessary."

"But the crew knows your place," Trecia said. "They would not confirm your story."

Joses smiled. "I am more clever than you give me credit for. I have already spoken with each man about this. They have all agreed that if we are overtaken, I become as one of them, and you two are merely passengers. They have also vowed to protect you and what you carry."

"No!" Phoebe said.

Joses came closer. "Be cautious of your tone and the heat in your voice. Why do you cry out like this?" He looked around, but it seemed to her that no one noticed their interaction. He sighed.

"You did not tell the crew what it is I am carrying, did you?" He shook his head.

"That is not sufficient, the wag of the head. Tell me in your own words," Phoebe said.

"No, of course not. You are carrying personal documents, that is all."

"Oh good," Phoebe said. "Thank you."

"But," Trecia said, "what story shall we connive around our documents?"

"That is up to the two of you," Joses said. "I should not know it for the safety of all of us. So with that, I will bid you goodbye." He returned to his work, and with his loss, Phoebe felt the absence of Albus all over again. There was something about missing a man. She had grown accustomed to being alone, to not needing a male voice, a steady companion. Though Joses did not hold a place in her heart as Albus did, it was his voice leaving that startled her into sadness.

"We can be city officials," Trecia said. "We represent Corinth on an important diplomatic mission."

"And why would they send a woman and her servant girl to do such a task?" Sometimes the simplicity of Trecia's thoughts stunned her, and not in a positive way.

She looked deflated after Phoebe's remarks, and Phoebe knew she had been the one to take the wind from her sails. "I am sorry. It may be plausible."

With that, Trecia smiled. "I have always wanted to become someone of import, but life has had its way of keeping me small and unnoticed. But now! I can be an official!"

Phoebe did not like this idea of deception. But then she remembered Rahab hiding the spies, a sort of divinely sanctioned "story" used to protect God's people, and she wondered if this type of falsehood was warranted. "I think we should finesse what we say so it more closely resembles the actual truth," she said. She thought for a moment, then a moment longer while silence grew between them. "We shall say these are tent designs." In a way, this was true. Paul had used the term "tent making" as a euphemism for planting churches, and the letter was, indeed, a skeleton framework for the church to hang its theology and practice on. Yes, this would be the outside story.

Trecia objected, "I would rather us be carrying treasure!"

Phoebe laughed. "If we told a story such as that, sea raiders would surely rob us of what little we have left. No, we stick to the tent story. Do you promise to hold true to it?"

"Yes," Trecia said. She put forward her hand, extending what Paul had called the right hand of the fellowship—a way to bind an oath.

Phoebe took it, then clasped both her hands around Trecia's. "You are the dearest person to me, save Paul. Thank you for endangering yourself for me. Thank you for showing me the sacrifice of Jesus in your actions. Thank you for loving me with such steadfast kindness. I do not know how I can repay you."

"A better story!" With this Trecia laughed. "I am jesting. We carry tent plans. No more. And in terms of repaying me? Your kindhearted patronage has been my salvation all these years. I am simply paying back the generosity you have bestowed graciously. I do not forget from where I came, the street I used to beg from, the pang of hunger in my stomach, the unquenched thirst that haunted me in Cenchreae after my parents' drownings. You rescued me, dear Phoebe. And it is my privilege to play a part of rescuing you."

CHAPTER FOURTEEN

After Trecia left, Phoebe remained under the sun's gaze. The words "play a part" reverberated through her. This was no play upon a stage, no joyful reenactment of false events. This was her life, her legacy. She prayed Trecia would finally understand the gravity of it all.

Someone touched her shoulder.

She leapt in the air, heart pounding, sudden terror springing to life within her.

"I am sorry to startle you," Joses said. "I called your name, but you did not hear me."

"It is fine. My mind was elsewhere."

He put his hands in the air as if in surrender. "I can see it upsets you. Please forgive me." With that, he returned to work, leaving her breathless, heart unsettled within her. Why did she react so violently to something so benign? But of course she knew. And the fact that Joses resurrected this wound made the remembering all the harder. Why did grief have a habit of revisiting its victims?

She hadn't always startled easily. She had been a steady girl, then woman, never affected by anything, it seemed, cocooned by the kindness of her parents and their relative ease in situation. Life felt blessedly normal and controlled as much as it could be in her status. Good life. Simple aspirations. Hope for the future. Then marriage.

With the deeply sad predicament of her empty womb graying their lives, all seemed to go well for her and Albus in other ways, particularly their relationships with their parents. But with the introduction of the nameless woman who laid a frail hand upon an even frailer ankle, the volcano of what was to come began its rumbling.

They sat nervously, she and Albus, in the courtyard of her parents' home. Albus's family had been invited too. Phoebe already knew their thoughts. They were expecting an announcement of progeny, that her womb had been filled at last with the hopes and legacies of both families. Mother flitted around, offering the hospitality that came so naturally to her. Wine, flatbread, goat cheese, honey—all expertly arranged on their central low-slung table. Cheerful conversation peppered the atmosphere, which only added to the sour feeling in her stomach. She knew this would be the pivotal moment, the fulcrum upon which everything would change. There would be life before the declaration—that predictable life—and their lives after, something she could not know, but feared. Apparently, rightly so.

She had always been a predictor of futures, though she often doubted her abilities. She was no prophetess, she knew. Hers was acuity for discerning people's faces, their temperaments, their intellectual choices, tossed with their upbringings. She could read people and therefore predict their next decisions. This had been her gift prior to knowing Christ, and it persisted afterward, though now she was much more cautious about using her predictions as a way to gain attention from others. She kept her thoughts to herself, mulling over them endlessly, which had resulted in much self-torture. As she sat quietly while others chatted in the dimming light of day, and as candles had been lit and placed on lampstands, she dreaded the next moments because she knew, really knew, what would happen.

Albus cleared his throat, garnering attention. "We wanted to gather to share something important with you," he said. His voice sounded resolute, steady. Phoebe went to his side, grabbing his hand for strength, but inside she shivered.

She nodded, noting her mother's expectant face. Yes, she wanted a grandchild—this was written all over her expression. All the faces turned her way registered joy. Soon they would reflect rage.

"You have taken note of my healed foot," Albus said simply. "We have not told you the entire story of my healing, just that it happened after we visited the shrine. What we didn't tell you was who healed me."

"It matters not the how or the who," Albus's father, Euneus, said. "The evidence of what happened makes us all happy." He spoke as a lawyer, which he was.

For what seemed like several minutes, Albus said nothing, adding to Phoebe's discomfort.

"It was Jesus," he finally said.

Silence answered back.

He squeezed her hand, while tears leaked from her eyes. She would stay steady, represent her Jesus well, but in the moment her earlier resolve felt flimsy.

"We met a woman—"

"So there is no child?" Mother snapped her interruption.

"No, I am sorry to say, we are not with child. But we met—"

"Why did you bring us here? To insult our gods—our family religion?" Mother's voice held wrath, Phoebe knew. She had given her life to the worship of her gods, and this mention of Jesus certainly rattled her.

"Not at all," Albus said. "If you let me finish." He motioned for all to recline at the table, which they did. He sat as well, Phoebe sitting next to him. "We met a woman who prayed for me."

"To which god did she pray?" This time the words came from Albus's mother. Hers was not a voice of anger but of deep sadness, as if she knew the answer already and had played out their inevitable response.

"As I said, she prayed in the name of Jesus Christ, the One known to be the crucified then resurrected Messiah. And at the mention of His name, my ankle suddenly sprang back to life, and I could walk and then dance. Phoebe is witness of this."

"It is as he says," she said, while her stomach continued its churning.

"And we have made a decision to follow this Jesus for the rest of our lives. We have joined a local community of the Way and will be baptized soon."

With all those declarations—conversion, following, the Way, baptism—Albus sealed their fate with the blood of Christ. There was no going back—only forward, and alone.

"You have tricked my daughter, bewitching her into a cult religion she knows nothing of. How dare you?" Father's words dripped as a snake's, with venom.

"He has not," Phoebe said. "It is as much my decision as it is his. We simply cannot deny the power of Jesus to heal him, nor can we blaspheme the Spirit who lives within us now. We have found joy, purpose, everything our hearts have searched for." The words sounded plausible upon her tongue, but when they escaped into the night air of the central atrium, they didn't reverberate. No, they fell flat.

"Are we not enough? Do you have any sort of allegiance to the ones who gave you life? For the gods' sake, we bent our will to let you marry this *man*." Father spit "man" from his lips as a curse word.

What more could be said? Would further explanation stem the waves of opposition? Would arguments cause either set of parents to understand the transformation that radically happened within them? Could they fashion the story a different way so as to welcome more understanding? Albus tried, reiterating the story in several different ways, but to no result except for an increasing hostility.

"Enough of this!" Father said. "You have said your words, and you have both made it clear that you want nothing to do with us, our customs, or our lives. You have betrayed everything we hold dear."

"But Father," Phoebe pled, this time with quavering voice, "I am your only child. Surely we can reason together."

He spat into his hands, rubbed them together, then shook them as if ridding them from himself. "I wash my hands of you, daughter. I am a childless man, and your mother is a woman with an unfilled womb—as you are right now. Perhaps your childlessness is a punishment from the gods for your disregard for them. I hasten to believe that to be true."

"No!" she wailed. Albus kept her hand in his, squeezing tightly. They had spoken of all the ways this conversation could go, but these words from her father represented the saddest case of all. Like Job, what she feared had come upon her, and her heart melted within her.

Father and Mother stood from the table. Albus's parents mimicked them.

His father said, "You must realize what you have done. Your words have created an uncharted rift between us. A phraseology of no return. My simple and last request is this: denounce this folk hero Jesus and gain some sense. If you gain Him, you lose us all. If you lose Him, you gain the world."

Albus stood. "'What good is it for someone to gain the whole world, yet forfeit their soul?' These are the words of our Savior, the One who died for the sin of humanity, then gloriously defeated death. He is my first allegiance. He warned that when people followed Him, they would sometimes have to leave family behind. That does not mean we cannot be family. In fact, I would say that His love for you burns within my heart in a passion I did not have before. I love you all more than when I lived beneath your roof. Oh that you would understand that following Jesus brings life."

"I cannot believe such dribble or sentiment," his father said. "Enough of your words. Enough of this supposed Jesus. I have heard the rumors, and they are credible, that He was a devil of a man, a mere charlatan whose followers concocted a resurrection story to keep their movement going. This is all deception, not truth. Please hear me. Please turn from Jesus and return to us." Albus's father wrung his hands, and his face reddened.

"I cannot. Phoebe cannot. We are steadfast in our commitment to Him."

Phoebe nodded as she took note of Mother's face, which looked paler than normal. She had battled a wasting disease for some time, but these words seemed to have purloined her last remaining health. Phoebe felt the weight of it all, as all four parents glared their way.

"You will leave now." The four words she expected from Father's mouth instead came from Mother's, which made them ever more emphatic as they echoed in the atrium.

This was it. The end. Albus sighed. He wrapped a cloak around Phoebe.

"We will love you until we breathe our last," he said. "And we will be praying for your souls, that someday you will come to understand this decision we have made."

"Do not patronize us, son," Albus's father said. "Leave our presence at once."

They obeyed the commandment to honor and obey their parents, at least in this last act. Sorrow collapsed upon Phoebe. She could feel the tension emanating from their parents as she and Albus turned to leave—to face an unknown future.

"Goodbye," she said, but no one answered back.

The next day in the throes of their grief Albus entered their chamber quietly and placed a hand upon her shoulder, and she startled for the first time. He apologized as Joses did today—truly sorry for surprising her, for upsetting her peace. The grief and the trauma of the interaction with her once-parents had unsteadied her, made her fretful and fearful, unmooring her. In her anguish, she often prayed just one word. *Jesus.*

Jesus.

Jesus.

She had abandoned her parents to follow Him. And although peace settled into the corners of her heart and she knew deep down that she had made the right choice, she had hoped that her anticipation of their rejection had been wrong, that her predictive abilities this time would have proven false. But no. She predicted their turning away, their abandonment. She had done so perfectly. And now everything she ever knew about parents and children and the love between both decayed. What had once been a dream now became a nightmare where she was left alone by the very people who should have protected and loved her for life. This was a sorrow indeed. And even as she reflected upon the story today under the sunshine, she shivered. There were some losses one never grew accustomed to.

CHAPTER FIFTEEN

The horizon where the ant-like ships had appeared like a tiny army now boasted closer boats. Phoebe worried afresh about their intent. Were they carrying people who had no good plans for them? She touched the satchel secured to her chest. How would she endure? Would she keep the story straight? *Tent plans,* she reminded herself. *These are merely new plans for new tents.*

Captain Regulus approached her, his right hand twitching. "You best be careful," he said.

"What do you mean?" The gulls above screeched joy, and the sun seemed to laugh. How could tragedy occur on a day that smelled so sweet?

"Normally I am not one to heed rumors, but it seems these are correct." He pointed to where the ants became grasshoppers. "See that one in the middle? The sail is taller than the rest?"

She squinted, then nodded. Yes, one tall mast supported a sail that dwarfed the other ships around it, though it was still hard to make anything out, what with her untrained seafaring eyes.

"I have encountered that ship years past. Roman officials arrested the crew about two seasons ago, but it looks as if they have resurrected themselves."

"Will they overtake us?"

"Hard to say with this weakened wind. But we will do our best to outrun them. Problem is, the race is a long one, a good eight days or so before we are scheduled to reach land. I can sprint and win, but to race that long may take its toll on us all. Best you pray to the gods for our safety, ma'am."

"I pray to only one God, and He made the seas."

Captain Regulus stroked his beard. "I have heard of people like you."

She expected disdain then but did not receive it.

"Is there not a tale of a man who incurred the wrath of his God while that God pummeled his ship? And only when he confessed to his crew that he was running hightail away from that God did the crew members reluctantly—and with great fear, I might add—pitch the man overboard? Some say the man drowned that very moment, but others tell of a giant fish swallowing the man whole, then vomiting him up on the beach."

"His name was Jonah," Phoebe said.

"Yes, I believe that to fit my recollections of the story. Seems the man who had been running turned around and ran toward the task his God mandated, to tell an unruly people about this God. The man did so, but the people rebelled. So much for listening to the voice of a god!"

The wind picked up. Phoebe grasped the handrail, wondering if she should correct the story. But as the tall-masted ship continued its gain, she realized He held everything in His hands, even this ship. May as well set the matter straight.

"Actually, the story goes that Jonah went to Ninevah and preached many days. And contrary to what you have heard, the whole city turned away from their wickedness. Where God would have destroyed them, He relented at their repentance."

"You suppose your rendering of the tale is true?" Captain Regulus cleared his throat, then spit over the rail. His spittle landed in the sea, swirling briefly then being absorbed by the waves.

"I know it is true."

"So Jonah, he must have been rejoicing. His message worked! I know I feel that way when all my men listen to me and obey every order."

"Actually, no."

"What do you mean?" The captain turned to look at her.

"He was upset. He seemed to want to serve a vengeful god. These people were his archenemies, and he longed for justice. When the nation turned from their ways, and God chose to pardon, Jonah became entirely upset. God even caused a vine to grow above him as he watched in expectation for the city to be destroyed. The day was hot, and he took joy in the shelter as he perched above what he thought was the best vantage point to the city's demise."

"But nothing happened."

A gull circled above, crying loudly. "Nothing happened. But when God caused the weed that had become a welcome shelter to wither, Jonah grew angry. Why did this shelter die? And that is when God reminded Jonah about His kindness. Jonah had compassion on a plant that withered, but God created the entire earth, including Ninevah and its inhabitants. Should He not be concerned for the people He created?"

"I suppose so, but I think I understand Jonah more than this god you speak of. He seems capricious, much like the gods of the seas—as one who changes his mind."

"You speak with long words, Captain."

With this he laughed. "People who man ships are not ignorant, madam."

"I am sorry. You are correct. I have never been on a ship before, so all this is new to me. I hope you can forgive me for implying your ignorance."

He laughed again. "I suppose I am like your god, Phoebe. I can forgive, or pardon, as you say. Especially one so beautiful." He placed his hand upon her forearm and kept it there.

And at that moment, Joses arrived. "Captain, what is your belief on the ship over yonder?"

He removed his hand from her arm, relieving Phoebe. Dangers did not merely lurk outside a ship. Because the ship housed fallible human beings, evil lurked everywhere. She suddenly felt small again, not up to the task Paul felt so confident about. How would she overcome so many obstacles? Trials without, fears within, her life suddenly felt like the wind above her, blowing chaotically without pattern.

In that meandering of thought, she caught the last bit of the captain's words before he walked away, something like "by nightfall."

She turned again toward the horizon where the ship with the tall sails had clearly pulled away from the conglomeration of ships. "Is it a ship of sea raiders?" she asked.

"I believe so. At least the captain says as much, though I am not sure if he says it for salacious reasons, to spin a good story, or if his voice is rendering a true verdict. I have a hard time reading his intentions."

"I am usually good at that kind of understanding," she said, her mind drifting back to the day her parents disowned her.

"What is your hunch?"

"I believe him."

Joses shook his head. "Remember what we have planned. You and Trecia keep your stories similar, and I will keep my distance working. However"—with this he bent nearer to her and lowered his voice—"I will always sleep in the same place above deck. You can always signal me if you feel you are in danger."

"Thank you," she said.

"But more than that. I will signal you too. Sea raiders usually do not board a ship in broad daylight, though I have heard that some brazen ones do. They sneak in at night when many except the watchmen slumber. I will alert you. I will keep watch."

"That does bring comfort, Joses."

"I am afraid I do not bring much comfort. I have many regrets in my life, many things I wish I could take back, but I can say this. God will watch over you. Yours is His mission."

She remembered, then, the psalm the apostle Paul often quoted when danger threatened. "I have a gift for you," she said.

"And what is that?"

"Words of comfort after all."

"I would much like to hear them," he said. Joses looked straight ahead at the ship that seemed determined to gain on them.

She pictured Paul then, speaking a comforting psalm. "'Out of the depths I cry to you, LORD; Lord, hear my voice. Let Your ears be attentive to my cry for mercy. If You, LORD, kept a record of sins, Lord, who could stand? But with you there is forgiveness, so that we can, with reverence, serve you. I wait for the LORD, my whole being waits, and in His word I put my hope. I wait for the Lord more than the watchmen wait for the morning, more than the watchmen for the morning. Israel, put your hope in the LORD; for with the LORD is unfailing love and with him is full redemption. He himself will redeem Israel from all their sins.'"

"It is a psalm I know well," Joses said. "Thank you for sharing that with me."

"Thank you for being a watchman during a tumultuous time." She hugged herself, feeling the parchment rolls beneath her arms as the wind caressed her skin.

"I fear I may not meet your expectations."

"It is not my expectations you must meet. Only the gaze of God matters. Only what He sees is of significance."

"Indeed." He continued his gaze toward the ship in the distance. "I have to trust God sees us here upon the seas."

Phoebe fell silent as the sun began its descent behind her. She remembered her recounting of Jonah's story. It had been one Paul had shared in the hearing of the gathering of believers in Cenchreae. He spoke it to spark a desire to share the

Good News with the whole world, not to decline the call of God, but to obey, come what may. Yes, God saw Jonah upon the seas. Although a reluctant prophet, he eventually bent to God's will, and in the end, an entire city was saved. Would this be the result of the scroll she hid? Would the church in Rome be spared much because of this one small effort? She thanked the Good Lord for considering her faithful, entrusting her with this service. Though the ship before them gained and gained, she knew that no man, no sea raider, no ship, no captain, no schemes of man, could ever thwart the high plans of God. He would pardon. He would redeem. He would prevail. This brought peace to her heart, though she knew that its fickle ways would soon be swayed again toward worry.

"All will be well," Joses said, but his unsteady voice betrayed such confident words.

"Yes, in the long run, it will." She thought of the coming kingdom, the glory that was to come, that what she did mattered here on earth, and she threw a prayer toward the gulls and the wind. *God in heaven, hear my prayer. Be the watchman over us all. Protect Your Word. Bring this parchment to its destination despite my fear. Bring us safely to port. Give me the words to speak when I am confounded and tongue-tied. I trust in Your Spirit within me to do such a miracle. I am scared. Yet I believe. I trust You. I need You. I honor You. I long for You. I hope in You. I revere You. I love You. I worship You. Amen, and so be it.*

CHAPTER SIXTEEN

Trecia mumbled in her sleep with the gentle sway of the boat under a midnight sky. Phoebe knew the hour, as she had spent much of her life battling sleeplessness, and her mind grew accustomed to night's schedules. While her servant had conversations with people unknown, Phoebe conversed with her heavenly Father, asking for strength again, hoping she would bear up under whatever trial befell her. It was one thing to know a trial and face it again. She would not want to walk through the first months of widowhood again, but she had experienced God's faithfulness so tangibly that she knew she could walk through loss again. Perhaps this was boastful pride speaking because there were moments when the grief felt like strangulation. Still, that would be a known tribulation. But sea raiders overtaking a ship? Completely foreign. And although she could make her way through the sea on a small boat if she had to, she knew land stood far, far away, and panic would most likely take over as the depths pulled at the tiny frigate.

She strained to hear anything from above, but Joses must have given in to slumber. All that filled her ears were the creaking of the ship, Trecia's voice, and the pounding of her fear, lodged in her chest.

Knock. Knock. Knock.

Oh no. What is it?

Three more knocks.

As she pulled her stola around herself and made sure the parchments were secure, she stood in the darkness on unsteady feet. Sailors' legs seemed to be created for the lulling of a boat's roll, but hers would never be. She tripped over her left foot, then steadied herself on a small ledge she knew to be eye level.

A rap came at the door to her cabin.

She opened it to Joses and a torch, his face illuminated scarily in the dark. "They are near," he whispered.

Trecia stirred but did not arouse.

"What are we to do?" Phoebe looked beyond Joses to see if the others were readying themselves for invasion. None stirred.

"I will alert all below, then return here. I will be needed in defending the ship. Do you have means to secure the door?"

She thought of the shelf, rickety and nearly off the wall. "Yes, I could bar the door."

"Good. There is little time. Pray to our God that He will bring us favor, will you?"

"I am in constant prayer, Joses. Please be safe."

He left Phoebe there. She watched as he ran down the corridor, hollering, knocking, then opening doors. "Sea raiders," he shouted. "Rouse yourselves, men!"

All at once cacophony reigned. Shouts, curse words, the clanking of swords punctuated the night while torches lit the ship's underbelly. They were like a hive of bees suddenly awakened and ready to sting.

The boat heaved violently to the left. Phoebe fell into her tiny room, toppling onto Trecia. The girl screamed, but Phoebe clamped her hand over her mouth. "Shh, we are being invaded."

"What?"

"Sea raiders have rammed the ship, I am certain. We must be quiet."

"God, please help us!" Trecia whispered.

"Help me secure our door." Phoebe grabbed Trecia's arm, directing her toward the shelf. "We will need to pull this from the wall, then barricade the door with it."

She silently assented to the task, while they pulled until the shelf broke free from the wall. Phoebe angled the board three quarters of the way up the doorway where the latch protruded, letting it angle toward the floor and the opposite wall. For all the internal complaint she had about the smallness of their quarters, tonight they were indeed a blessing. With the door wedged as it was, sea raiders would have to hack through the door with an ax in order to get to them. She prayed they'd consider it a storage closet, nothing more, then move on.

Above them, the chaos intensified from calm to boot steps. Shouts and grunts peppered the night. She grabbed Trecia's hands in hers as they prayed quietly—no words between them, but hundreds of words shot through the ceiling toward the heavens in hopes of salvation from this terror.

She remembered the day being calm, no clouds in the sky, so when something dripped on her head from above, she wondered what it could mean. Was it raining? Had God sent a storm to thwart the onslaught? But when she felt a drop between her fingers and brought it to her nose, the smell of copper shared a difficult truth—blood. Blood spilled above them, dripping on them. She wanted to tell Trecia but thought the better of it since she frightened easily, and theirs was a tenuous safety. Silence would be their hope. No use in adding to the terror.

The melee continued for seconds upon minutes upon an hour, and then much was quieted. She could hear the voice of Captain Regulus briefly but then could not distinguish the voices above her. She remembered the stories of rape at the hands of sea raiders, wondering if she and Trecia were being bartered in exchange for the boat's freedom. She wiped her eyes of blood while Trecia trembled beside her. They clasped hands, both cold and clammy, but Trecia kept one hand clamped over her mouth, as if she knew if she pulled it away, a cry would escape. Phoebe shushed her, but not in the way a mother scolds a child. She hoped it would be a welcome soothing noise that would calm Trecia and herself without raising suspicion beyond the doorway.

For several hours they stayed alert like that, while boots tromped above them, voices rose and fell, until, finally, light came through the slats above them. That's when Trecia saw the blood upon Phoebe's face and nearly screamed, but Phoebe covered her mouth just in time. She shook her head no, put her finger to her lips to convey, "Silence."

A sheepish knock came at the door. Then louder. The pounding of it echoed Phoebe's heartbeat that moved from her chest to her neck. She could barely swallow, the terror had so consumed her. A scuffle erupted behind the door, causing her to pray. She asked God to remind her that this life was not all there was, that what she did here on earth mattered for eternity, and if she suffered for His sake, then He would receive more glory and she would have died trying to complete such an important task. She wanted to force herself to believe this would get rid of any fear, but she trembled all the more as the noise behind the door intensified and then silenced. Their makeshift shelving wedge held the door blessedly shut.

It was at this moment she realized something. They could not stay in this room for all those days, particularly since she did not know where they would head if sea raiders had commandeered the vessel. They would need water, and they had none.

"Phoebe!"

The voice of Joses.

Trecia grabbed her forearm and shook her head no.

Was this a trap?

But if they stayed in the bloodied darkness of this room, they would perish. So she removed the wood and opened the door as Trecia's fingernails dug into her arm.

Joses did stand there, yes, but so did an unfamiliar man with dark eyes.

"Ma'am," Joses said, his voice formal.

Phoebe could see by his stare that they were to play along with this formal charade, so she simply nodded.

"I am sorry I did not come sooner. As you can imagine, things have been a bit chaotic."

A man approached Joses from behind.

"We are continuing on to Rome, thanks to this new captain. Meet Stavros."

Stavros bowed slightly before them.

Phoebe wondered what a sight they must be, bloodied and harried. She did not know whether to speak or not.

"I am sorry for the inconvenience," he said, his voice thickly accented from the East. "But this man tells me you are merely passengers on your way to Rome, is that correct?"

She wondered if he noticed the satchel strapped to her, and still fell mute.

"Yes," Trecia said.

"I have no business with you, then. This man says you are protected by forces greater than I, though I run by my own code. Yet he makes his point emphatic that you are not to be trifled with in any way."

"Are we prisoners, then?" Phoebe finally asked.

"A matter of semantics. Are we not all prisoners to Rome? Do they not control us all, take our livelihoods, kick us when we have gained a hairbreadth of power? All you need to know is that this ship is captained by me, and we will deport near Rome. Am I clear?"

"Perfectly," Phoebe said. "We are thirsty. Are we permitted to drink? May we clean ourselves?"

"I have asked this man to accompany you wherever you go." He pointed to Joses. "You are free to take care of needs, but he must be with you."

Phoebe nodded. "Thank you."

Stavros turned on his boot and ventured toward the ship's center. Joses waited several moments before he spoke. "Be utterly cautious," he said.

"What happened?" Phoebe asked.

"Let us speak in your quarters." Joses pointed to their tiny room.

Once inside, he pointed toward the ceiling where blood still dripped. "They arrived as you must have heard, with the ramming of our ship."

"Is Longinus alive?" Trecia asked.

"I do not know. But the ship is seaworthy still, and Regulus has been spared, though he is in chains in the galley. I am unsure if there will be a counteruprising, though that could be a possibility." He kept his voice barely audible, so much so that Phoebe had to place her ear nearly on his mouth.

"This man Stavros is greedy, to be sure, but that seems to be his primary motivation. Yes, he shed blood, but it was as minimal of a takeover as I have heard of. If we were to be overtaken by sea raiders, his ship is perhaps the more benevolent one."

"I am frightened," Trecia said.

"This is a frightening turn of events." Joses kept his voice down. "But we are not without resources. God is with us. Our mission is important. And we have been granted surprising favor in the eyes of this scoundrel. I do not know how long his mercy will last, or even if it is an act. So you must be on your guard. Do not ever do anything without me by your sides. Are we perfectly clear on this?"

"Yes," Phoebe said.

Trecia said nothing, seemingly lost in her thoughts.

"You are bloodied. Let me accompany you toward the open air. You will find the ship relatively unchanged, save the flag that flies above it. Do not speak to anyone you do not know. Do not engage them. Keep your eyes down and your manner meek."

"I thought you were going to stay away from us," Phoebe said. "Let us alone in our tent-making story."

"I do not know why, but once Stavros knew I was a former slave, I found favor with him. It must have been Providence who prompted me to say such a strange admission on a night of unsteady violence. From that moment on, he spoke of the beauty of emancipation that the sea provided. All men, he said, are free upon the sea. It was then I took the opportunity to tell them of you. The tent story will still work, but we can be linked together, and I feel better knowing I will be in a place to protect you."

"This is good news," Phoebe said. "Thank you for bending to the will of the Almighty in what must have been a frightening situation."

"Jesus promised words to those who needed it, and Paul said just as much. That when we are fearful of what we are to say in a difficult situation, the Spirit will give us proper utterance. I give the Spirit all the credit, as my nature would have been to stick to our original plan. God knows far more than we do, and *His* plan is far more intricate and beautiful than we could ever imagine. It is worth learning how to bend an ear toward the Spirit's whispers, correct?"

Phoebe nodded.

The three staggered toward the light, while new men, smelling of sweat and drink, watched them closely. Phoebe felt their leering and once again worried that she would become fodder for their nighttime pursuits. She threw another prayer heavenward asking God to please protect them all while she washed the blood from her hair, face, and hands.

CHAPTER SEVENTEEN

Days played upon the sea.
Dawn.

Midday.

Dusk.

Inky night.

And all appeared to be unchanged, except for the crew. They continued their quest toward Rome to make their journey swift. Apparently, Longinus survived the onslaught and managed to curry favor with the sea raiders as they discussed the best manner of finalizing their trip to Rome. To Phoebe's mind, the boy was as slippery as a sea lion in his loyalties, giving allegiance to anyone who paid him. But to Trecia, he was noble, and she stayed in rapt connection with him despite Phoebe's consistent warnings. The only good that came of her obsession was this—Trecia reported everything she heard back to Phoebe. "The wind is good, they say. Instead of hugging the land, they will put out farther to sea, avoiding the dangers of the shore. It is as if nothing has happened, other than the interruption in captains."

Phoebe tried to stand in their cramped quarters, lifting their bucket of waste to be disposed of. It was her turn to hurl the contents to the sea, a vile job but necessary to keep the flies away. Though technically Trecia's job, she had volunteered to shoulder the load as part of her desire to follow Jesus's words about the greatest in the kingdom becoming a servant. "Much has happened, Trecia. And things are not as they were. I fear danger. Please keep your connection to Longinus chaste and appropriate." She pushed through the doorway, excrement bucket in hand.

"Of course. Remember who it is you speak to, dear Phoebe. I too have heard Paul preach on chastity and the necessity of being wholeheartedly devoted to Jesus Christ. You have forgotten, perhaps, that God works in mysterious ways. Maybe I am in this relationship for greater purposes."

"Well, I hope that is true. My purpose now?" She made a face at the odor she carried. "To dispose of our waste."

"Carry on, brave one," Trecia said, laughing.

Phoebe prayed that no one would see her as she scaled the ladder toward the graying sky above her. But, alas, Joses stood there. He lifted the humiliating bucket from her as she ascended and whisked it away and over the ship before she could protest. As she neared him, he lowered the bucket by a rope back to the sea, capturing salty water within. He hauled it upward, swished it around, tossed the water, and then returned it to the sea. He did this three times to cleanse it, as he said.

"Thank you," Phoebe said.

"Speak no further of it."

"Is all well today?"

"Our wind is genial, and it woos us swiftly. We may make up time along the way. This actually may bode in our favor."

"You sound like Trecia. I am not so sure. How can having a ship overtaken become a good thing?" With this she lowered her voice, looking around, but none of the new crew seemed to take notice of her. "Are you sure they are safe?"

"Not one person is safe. I am not safe. We are all beset with sin, Phoebe." With this, he laughed—a rare thing for a man so serious.

"Of course I know that, but I tend to view people in categories. Do you not do that as well?"

"My whole life has been categories. Slave. Free. Those who have freedom. Those who do not. The hungry. The satisfied. But now upon this sea? I see things differently. Is that not what Paul has preached? There is neither slave nor free?"

"Nor male or female," she reminded him.

"It is as you say. So I do not think of sea raiders as lawbreakers, though they are. But I see them as mere men."

"But what of obedience? What of Jesus separating sheep and goats at the end of time? Does it not matter what people do? Should we not fear God?"

"According to Paul, we should always fear God, but we should never presume to play Him. We cannot know the intentions of the heart."

Phoebe felt the wind on her face. It had a tinge of coolness to it, and she welcomed the breeze after such a stench-filled night. "No, but we can easily discern the heart by actions."

"People are more complicated than that."

His words begged a response, but she had none, perhaps because they rang true.

Joses left a moment, then returned with water. "You need to remember to drink. The air is dry."

She took the water to her lips and let it slake her thirst—something she didn't realize she had. "Would you permit me to ask you how I should conduct myself regarding this?" She pointed to the satchel.

"Wearing it brings suspicion. If I were you, I would hide it under your palla in your quarters. We will not be much longer upon the seas, and from what I hear on the deck, these men are merely interested in selling the goods quickly, then departing. They have no compelling longing for scrolls or any such thing."

"I am unsure if I should let them out of my sight. Trecia, she is—"

Stavros approached them. It was his cough that announced his arrival. "Excuse me," he said. "Is all well for you, ma'am?"

"Yes, thank you. Do you have an estimate for Rome?"

"Nigh four days and we will be ashore. And then you can safely disembark."

"Disembark is a good word," she said. "I do not think I will ever have sea legs as the rest of you." At this several gulls cried above them, as if adding an exclamation to her claim.

"The sea can topple a person's stomach—and it does so to me at extraordinarily stormy times," the new captain said.

She nodded. Her own stomach had revolted many times.

Joses turned to Stavros. "Whatever you need, Stavros, let me know. I have learned over the years how to live without sleep. I can keep watch and stay awake when most men's eyes are lidded and heavy."

"That is a good quality. My men tend toward sleepiness, particularly in the later watches of the night." He turned to Phoebe. "Be cautious, my lady. I would like to think I keep all men tame, but no man can wrangle another, as you may well know. Stay near to myself or Joses here, and all will be well."

She worried at his words while the wind whipped her hair from its confines. She tried to tuck it beneath her palla, but the *fibulae* holding it secure wavered in the breeze. Errant hair. Errant people. With that thought, she felt the stirring of the Spirit within her to speak. She cleared her throat. "I will certainly abide by your advice, but I must tell you where my deepest security rests. It does not rest upon land or landfall. It does not rest in a journey that sees success. It does not rest in wealth or a healthy countenance. It does not rest in the protection of men. It rests firmly upon one Rock."

"As a sea captain," Stavros said, "I am not one who enjoys rocks."

"I understand," Phoebe said. "But you would do well to place your confidence on this Rock—that of the Lord Jesus Christ, the Prophet and King who died for our selfishness and resurrected to prove His deity. He alone is my protector and confidant." She felt strength rise to her voice.

"I have heard stirrings of stories like this. But I have sailed many seas, encountered dangers everywhere I have embarked. And, truth be told, I have created my own danger. There are cults and sects alike. I see the fleeting nature of them all. They are wind, here today, absent the next. They storm in like thunder and die out in a whimper. No, ma'am, I appreciate your adherence to something that makes you feel better, but I will not bow to a deity. I am my own deity. I, alone, am the person I can trust. Surely you understand a sentiment such as this?" He coughed again, this time more consumptive, while Joses fetched water and handed it to him.

"You," Stavros said, motioning to Joses. "You believe this woman's superstitions?"

"It is as you say." Joses's voice was strong, despite the wind becoming shriller in the sail above.

Stavros laughed. "Ah, another man bewitched by a woman, I see. You? A slave? I suppose I can understand it, then. Your owner, did he share this same belief? And were you required to keep it?"

Joses did not speak in response. Instead he hummed.

"How convenient to cease speaking." Stavros laughed, which caused his cough to rear its angry bark. Once the cough stopped, he winked at Joses. "I understand. You will soon abandon a master's god when you have created more distance between you and him. The farther away you sail, the less grip that mysticism will have on you. Mark my words, Joses. With Rome in sight, your so-called faith will dissolve. I have seen it many years in my life upon the waters."

Phoebe wanted to step in and defend Joses, but she realized she knew him about as well as this stranger did. Perhaps Joses was playacting it all, creating an elaborate facade of a freed slave who loved Jesus. Did not Paul warn about false teachers and false apostles? Did he not call them dogs? Would Joses withstand scrutiny if pressed? Would he truly follow Jesus to the ends of the earth? This, she could not know. So she kept silent while the wind continued its relentlessness and the gulls called from the sky above. Four more days. That was all she needed to endure. The three of them would locate Priscilla and Aquila. She would deliver the manuscript with her words but with the emphatic elocution of Paul, then set about to pay for copies to be made. If she kept her mind on these tasks, her mind would stop its wandering into speculating disaster.

Stavros left them. Joses returned her bucket. She felt the flush in her cheeks. "Thank you," she said.

"I will not leave you, Phoebe."

His words sounded rote to her, as if they were rehearsed. Her heart shifted in that moment. Was the turning away because she loved Jesus or because she had been betrayed so many times and her caution was warranted? Hard to discern. But she understood what Stavros said. While she would trust God, she still battled His call to trust other believers. In the past, her trust in others was severed in several ways—when her parents and husband's parents turned from them, when Albus's body sank into the soil—and that trust would most likely not resurrect, particularly when so much depended upon this mission. She reminded herself of Paul standing tall in her memory. She could trust him, but others? Though she knew that the hearts of men and women were bent toward wickedness, she had also seen sheer altruism burst forth from the Corinthian believers around her. Phoebe finally said, "I am grateful you will not abandon us both." And she determined to mean the words.

As she descended the ladder, she heard voices in the distant corridor—those of Trecia and someone else—was it Longinus?

"A talisman, right? Magic? Do you promise it?"

"Yes, very much so," came the male voice. "You long for power, right? This will give you the power you crave. The incantations will make you strong, secure your fortune, and provide your future."

What?

"Trecia," Phoebe said into the darkness of the ship's bowels.

Shifting and scuttling answered back.

"Trecia, is that you?"

"Yes ma'am," came her voice, quieter, less assured than it had been when Phoebe overheard her.

"Come here."

Trecia returned, unkempt, eyes wide, hair trailing from her palla. "What is it?"

"What were you talking about?"

"Oh, nothing." She paused. "Longinus bends toward the fantastic, and to alleviate boredom we have decided to create a story. So every time we have a moment, we add to it. It helps pass the time on the ship."

Longinus appeared, equally unkempt. "She is correct, ma'am. We are simply making up stories together. Nothing more."

Phoebe's gut told her there was more. Much, much more. "If you will excuse me, I would like to talk to Trecia alone."

He nodded and then departed toward the daylight above.

In their small room, Phoebe looked at Trecia, noting her beautiful face under the slats of daylight. "You must be careful," she said. "I do not think that man has honorable intentions with you. And your attention toward him may give the wrong impression."

"We are simply friends," Trecia said, her voice quiet.

"He looks at you as a husband admires a wife, Trecia. Surely you understand this is not proper. Your allegiance is first to God, then to me. And in light of that, I have to ask you not to spend time with this man any longer."

"But—"

"I cannot say it more firmly. He only wants to use you or take advantage of your naivety. Do not give in to girlish flirtations!"

"What do you have to say to such things? You are privileged. You can go where you want to go, stay when you want to stay. Me? I am bound to you. My life is tied inextricably to yours. I have no voice, no say, no ambitions but yours. Have you ever thought what it must be like for someone like me in this empire?"

Phoebe leaned back, letting out her breath. She had heard of insubordination of servants before, but had never experienced the phenomenon with Trecia. Paul had preached about how masters were to treat their slaves, with dignity and respect. But he also said to remain as you were if you were a slave. To serve with diligence as if serving the Creator. These words sounded foreign, and perhaps they were. Maybe Longinus had placed subversive ideas in her vulnerable servant's mind. "I have nothing to say in response. This is how our worlds work."

"No, this is how *your* world works. Have you considered life from my perspective? There are more people on this earth than yourself." Trecia's words seemed to be spat, not said.

Was Phoebe being so harsh? Had she placed an unfair burden upon Trecia's shoulders? "Of course I know that. You are deeply important to me. I consider you my companion, my friend."

Trecia said nothing for a long time.

From above their heads, footsteps rushed here and there. Sailors attended their duties while the silence between the two grew longer, emphasizing the chasm between them.

Phoebe finally said, "Are you with me? Will you finish this task alongside me?"

"That is what I plan on doing. Of course." But her voice sounded deflated.

Phoebe moved closer as she threw a prayer heavenward. The complicated nature of relationships confounded her at times. But she did know that Trecia had been her closest confidant when her husband passed. She had walked the road of grief with her. Theirs was not a superficial relationship based only on money exchanging hands for services rendered. Still, perhaps she had been unfair. What would Jesus have her do in this situation? An idea came to her. She cleared her throat. "Look at me, Trecia."

Trecia obliged.

"I have not sought the Lord about this, but when we are finished with our mission, I will see to helping you find a more suitable occupation—one that provides for you without having

118

to serve only my interests. Certainly within the church, there are opportunities for you, if that is what you desire. Is that your intent?"

Trecia placed her face in her hands then began to cry. Gulping in air, she wept and wept and wept. "You have done so much for me."

"Possibly not enough. You are right. I have not seen things from your perspective."

"Thank you for saying that."

"My words to you today in the corridor, I hope you know, come from a place of love. I worry about you being poisoned by talk that does not include the Lord Jesus. Please consider that Longinus does not have your best in mind."

Quiet settled between them. Trecia shook her head, as if trying to rid herself of thoughts. "You are right," she said finally. "Longinus has been driving a wedge between us with his words. I am sorry. I see that now. I will do better. I will accompany you wherever you go. I will be Ruth to you, my Naomi. But please do not speak of this to anyone."

Phoebe placed her hands on Trecia's shoulders, her heart melting. "Who would I tell? We only know Joses. I should think he would shy away from such talk. Are you in agreement about that?"

Trecia nodded. She wiped away her tears, pulled in a long breath, and then smiled. "Where would I be in this world without you?"

CHAPTER EIGHTEEN

Phoebe relieved herself of the satchel's burden. Joses's advice seemed sound, as she had noticed several of the new sailors eyeing her peculiarly as she wore it like armor across her chest. She did not tell Trecia of her hiding place, though it would not take her long to discover such a cache. There was only so much space in their tiny room. Come morning, she rose to pray, noting Trecia's strange absence. Where was the girl?

She heard something at her doorway and then felt compelled by the Spirit to lay her head back down. With one eye opened, she noted Trecia sneaking past her, to return to "sleep." Phoebe lay there several moments, pondering what to do. Should she possess the bravery of Paul, she would be blunt, confronting Trecia that very moment. But something held her back. Was it fear? Was she afraid of betrayal once again? No, she told herself, Trecia was trustworthy. She was her servant, her loyal companion—not only in occupation but also in matters of faith. Trecia must have felt sick—she had battled the seasickness of late—and spent time above deck under Joses's watchful care. She would ask him about it later. In the meantime, she spent her mock sleep in prayer—this time praying fervently for the congregation she left behind in Cenchreae.

Their fellowship felt both strong and tenuous, full of love and battles aplenty. By name she prayed for all the Lord brought to mind, asking that He would strengthen her friends to love well, find deeper wisdom in the things of God, chase after Jesus Christ in every endeavor, fight the good fight, understand the wily ways of the enemy of their souls, and serve each other with gladness and sincerity. She prayed for unity. She prayed for strength amidst inevitable persecution. And when she said amen in her heart, the burden of caring for those left behind lifted a bit. She wondered how Paul could carry so many congregations upon his shoulders, daily bearing the burden of the churches. It was something he seemed to do with joy, but she saw the strain behind his eyes. He was one who gave everything for the cause of Christ, she knew. So as she stirred a bit to rouse Trecia, she prayed again for the mission at hand, touching the place where the scrolls sat beneath her. God would keep them safe. He had to.

In the morning's quiet, she allowed her mind to wander far afield, to the places she sometimes avoided—that paradox of trust. It seemed God asked followers to trust Him implicitly, as an outworking of faith—even when circumstances shouted against it. But what of other people? She could make the case for trusting a good God, but what of an unkind humanity? And why would it matter if she always chose distrust over trust when it came to people?

Phoebe remembered one such conversation.

Paul had paced her courtyard, seldom one for sitting. His were the hands of one who constructed tents, and he did so with fury in order to provide for his journeys far and wide. That had instilled in him a restless busyness, a need to always be fidgeting, moving, creating, producing. So as she spoke, he walked back and forth as if he were avoiding an arrow's trajectory.

"Why does God value trust so much?" Phoebe's question, to her, seeped paradox. Trust God? Yes. Trust the people He made? Why did that matter?

"We know that without having faith, we cannot please God," came Paul's measured response, though his wink her way indicated he had only just begun his verbal adventure.

"Yes, I know that," she said, tracing her hand along the table before her. It had a scar along its top, marred when it had been a tree. She thought it beautiful, though her husband thought it broken. There had always been something instilled in her from the beginning, something God must have wrought that caused her to lean toward the flawed. The marring of the wood, however, did not compromise its ability to welcome guests. "God calls us to trust Him in every instance. But what about trust between people? Should you grant trust without discernment?"

"That is a compelling question," Paul said, continuing his pacing.

A bee buzzed through the roses in the courtyard, loud and insistent. Why she remembered that, she did not know, but it had seemed significant at that moment. Perhaps it represented the relentless existence of humanity's untrustworthiness in this world. Or perhaps it was just a bee kissing flowers. "What do you do when someone has violated your trust?"

Paul walked back to her, his eyes intent on hers. "I appreciate your question," he said. "And I dignify it. You are not one to simply be satisfied with simple questions, milk for your faith. No, yours is a longing for meat. That is why you are a respected deaconess in this body—your thirst for the deeper things of God will be rewarded. You are as Mary of Bethany, who took the position of a student, sitting at the feet of Rabbi Jesus. She worshipped Jesus as no other. She trusted Jesus. She waited in expectation. She helped in spreading the Good News of Him all over the world. Or you are as the Samaritan woman Jesus conversed with at the well. Peter has told me Jesus had the longest conversation of spiritual import with that woman. And she became as us—a missionary to many. She found the living water, spilling it gloriously onto others. You are in their vein, dear Phoebe. A woman of thought and a woman of action. I commend you."

She tried not to blush. She felt no romantic attachment to Paul, nor did she experience any sort of reticence that she did in the marketplace once the word *widow* became her moniker. The men there leered. But Paul? He simply listened. "You have not answered my question."

"Like any good teacher, I will respond in kind—with a question. What does wisdom tell you?"

"To flee from fools, yet convey trust to the wise."

Paul sat across from her, the scarred table between them. "Yes, it is as you say. But the Spirit is the deciding factor. He gives us the necessary discernment, showing us when to walk away, when to approach, when to be cautious, when to shake the dust from our feet."

"I wish there was a simple answer."

"As do I, dear Phoebe. It seems easier to trust our Creator but so much more complicated to trust those bent toward sin." Paul's forehead perspired.

Phoebe fetched some wine and handed him a cup.

"But what if someone has repeatedly harmed you or completely disowned you—like my parents?"

"To those who walk away, unless the Spirit specifically instructs you to do so, you have to let them go, praying that reconciliation may occur. And always pray that your heart tenderizes to His grace so that if your parents return to you, bitterness will not prevent that reconciliation."

The buzzing bee circled above them, then settled into the table's crack, seemingly resting. "It's hard to know the place between bitterness and plain old pain."

"True, but I have to look at all of this heartache in the context of the kingdom of God, right?"

She nodded, then shivered though the sun kept them warm, while the lazy bee continued to rest. Was it dead? Would it fly again? Would she? "Above all, I long to see the kingdom."

"As do I—and that means fully placing our trust in God and trusting Him with our relationships."

"Does it mean I am not trusting if I still hurt from my parents' turning away?"

"No, it means you loved well. Grief comes on the heels of love."

"That's a beautiful way to look at it," Phoebe said.

"You bear the scars, I know," Paul said. "But your scars are also badges of honor. You were considered worthy to suffer for Jesus."

"I know," she whispered. "But that honor does not erase pain."

"That is true." He stood. "But one thing I can say is this: God is trustworthy. Consider me. He changed the trajectory of my life. I was hell bent, but He bent to earth, shattered my darkness by a great light, blinded me for a time—which was a metaphor for my entire life up until that point—and chose me, the least of all, to proclaim His power to the Gentiles, a once-hated race, at least according to us Jews. He certainly transformed my hatred into love, my vengeance into compassion, my wrath into meekness. This is the work of the God who longs to see the whole world repent and come to the knowledge of Jesus Christ. I am utterly humbled and flummoxed by such a thing."

"Yours are eloquent words," she said.

"They are simply my story." He commenced his pacing.

"I suppose it is wrong for me to place myself in the sandals of God, to reduce trust to a formula."

"God's plan," Paul said, "is both mysterious and simple."

"And my part in it?"

"The same, dear Phoebe. I do not presume to know what it is at this point, but I feel a stirring from the Holy Spirit that He will ask you to do an important work. It will not be heralded by earthly friends or foes, but it will be seen in heaven. Be sure you are preparing your heart for whatever He entrusts you to."

"I am not sure-footed. My faith sometimes feels small."

"I am confident of this one thing, friend, that He who began that work of faith in you and Albus will complete it until the day of Christ Jesus. Your husband? He has completed his work, but yours is continuing. Be careful that you do not shrink back."

She sighed. The loneliness she felt in that moment she could taste and see and smell—that was how tangible it seemed. She sensed that any endeavor God would call her on would involve further isolation and persecution. To be honest, she wearied of it all. "I will not shrink back." As she said the words, the bee roused itself in resurrection, circled around Paul, then her, and landed upon her left wrist. She tried to bat it away, but it answered back with its stinger. Phoebe stood up. She cried out as she winced.

Paul asked, "May I?"

She nodded.

Scratching with his fingernails, he extracted the stinger. "Put some cool water upon it at once. You will be fine."

The memory of their bee sting meeting faded as the sun broke through the slats above, one ray angling down upon her scar—the place where the bee's sting wounded her, inflamed, infected, and hardened for months. Sometimes the words of others lasted, at least in the mind of the one harmed. Sometimes their sting lingered. Nevertheless, she would persist—through loneliness, through persecutions, through disasters, through sea raiders, through storms, through the great unknown. This world was not all there was, this place pivoting between the now and the not yet.

Dear God, she prayed. *I need Your Spirit's guidance. Who do I trust? Please protect me from enemies. But more than that, protect the scrolls beneath me. Honestly? I am terrified. But I am also resolute. I do pray that You would graciously complete the work You began in me until that Day. Help me to remember the words of Paul, that when I am weak, I am paradoxically strong because of You within me, giving me the power to work and do good deeds. You are the reason I lie here in this darkened cabin longing for Rome. Do not leave my side. I am nothing without You. This I pray with all sincerity and faith. I trust You. Please help my unbelief. Amen.*

CHAPTER NINETEEN

Prayers were a fickle practice, Phoebe decided. Because once she let out her anxieties before the Almighty, she birthed twins—peace and chaos. The peace God flooded her heart with was immediate, but the chaos bit on its heels. And not only bit but drew blood.

"We are going to port," Joses said, his eyes wide. "This is an unexpected stop, and I do not know what to make of it."

But Phoebe had learned enough about the man that his face told tales his voice did not. She saw fear there. "But to Rome? Will this lengthen our trip?" The air outside smelled different, more sea-like, as if seaweed and gull droppings were more intense.

Joses pointed in the distance. "There. Can you see it?"

She strained in the dimming light. The day had been a flurry of activity that had made little sense to her. Why all the bustling around? But at the end of Joses's trajectory she saw the horizon, no longer endless as the sea. Land emerged as if from a mist. She felt both comfort and fear at the sight of it. "So it is not Rome? You are sure? It has been a few days."

"Neapolis," he said, as if that should explain all mysteries for all times. He offered nothing more than a deep breath, let out far too long.

"No, it cannot be."

"I am afraid it is. Stavros never intended to complete the Roman voyage. And in the light of things, it makes sense to me. Why would he go to the port this ship was destined to sail to? Would he not be arrested for selling what is not his? But he knows scoundrels on the shore of Neapolis, best as I could discern from the hushed conversations above deck. He will disembark there, selling our cargo, then leave for another place. I am not sure of the ways of sea raiders. One would think they would continue to command the vessel they overtook, but that does not seem to be the plan of Stavros. Sell and move on, I would say."

"But what of us? Our mission?"

"We will have to hire another ship. Or travel from Neapolis to Rome on foot." His voice sounded resolute, but his demeanor shrank away, as if he was as tired as the relentless sea.

Phoebe let the wind torment her hair, not trying to retrieve it from her palla. What did it matter, propriety? Everything had been turned from purpose to uncertainty as the ship's sail pointed them toward the shoreline. How long would it be until they were in port? She tried to calculate her funds, wondering if she had enough to hire yet another ship. Even if they chose to fast, she had very little left. "I do not know what to say."

"Neither do I."

A large wave crashed against the ship, splashing her face and dress, but she did nothing to react. The coldness kept her alive, but it also felt like a slap from the Almighty. Where was His plan in such chaos as this? Would she be able to make the trek to Rome on foot? How would they lodge along the way? And how would she possibly protect the scrolls from roadside bandits so legendary on the Roman roads? Tears answered back, finally, to the former wave's onslaught. Usually she would care a great deal that she put on a strong front. Being a deaconess in a burgeoning church caused her to bend that way when trials and gossip and worries pressed in on her. But now? She did not care about what Joses thought. Her spine, once strong like the mast of their ship, quivered like a jellyfish that so beautifully glided in the waters beneath her. No backbone. No hope. All that peace God brought now dissipated through wave upon wave of worry.

They stood there feeling the shock of wind, wave, and land together, saying nothing but communicating everything. What lay next would be a mystery. Adventure was the wrong word to describe it. More like trepidation and uncertainty. But had this not been what Paul had warned her about when he went into detail about his own trials? Had he not been tortured for the sake of Jesus? Had he not been imprisoned? Beaten with rods? Exhausted? Did he not battle sickness while his eyesight deteriorated? His were not persuasive words, and his exploits, though sounding heroic in retrospect, must have been terrifying in each moment. She was no Paul. That she knew. But they shared the same Holy Spirit, as did Joses and Trecia. She had to remind herself that He would not walk away. While her parents abandoned her, He would not. While her husband passed, He would not. While her hopes were dashed as surely as the shore neared, He would remain utterly steady, alongside her as a companion and friend. She breathed in the scent of land, wiped away the tears, and said, "It will work out just as God has planned it to. It does us no good to fret. This is not what we anticipated, but none of it surprises our God."

"Thank you for that reminder," Joses said. "Our God has the ability to make a way through the thickest wildernesses."

"Even if the wilderness poses as the sea?" She smiled.

Joses laughed. "Yes. And even through the sea wilderness, be assured. I will be with you in this journey. No matter what happens, I will help you. Come what may."

Stavros interrupted their conversation. "We will be ashore soon."

"And what are we to do?" Phoebe did not hide her irritation.

"What is that to me? Am I your caretaker? You should be grateful nothing befell you under my watch. Believe me, I prevented much danger."

"Should that make me happy?" Phoebe pointed to shore. "That is not my destination. I have business in Rome."

"Oh yes," Stavros said. "You are bringing tent plans, correct? What I want to know is why do these plans mean so much? Surely there are only a few ways to create a tent. Are yours revolutionary?" He laughed.

Joses put his hand upon the shoulder of the captain, but Stavros shrugged it away. "Do not touch me."

Joses put his hands up as if in surrender. "Sorry. But I am worried about our future, how we will get to Rome. I know you are not inclined to help us, but we need passage, and soon, before the seasons change and sea passage becomes untenable."

"You are right in that regard. I will tell you this. Once I leave the ship and get what is mine, I will unchain Regulus. Perhaps he will hire new recruits, replacing who was lost—"

"You mean killed? I believe that is the precise word." Joses steadied himself with both hands on the railing.

"Yes, it is as you say. Killed. There are many sailors in want of a job in Neapolis, so he should not have much trouble securing a new crew."

"His livelihood, I believe, is the cargo he carried. He will need another payload, is that not right?" Phoebe did not hide her anger. She balled her fists, telling herself not to lash out, not to resort to hysterics. All of this crew gathering and goods finding would take time, and they had little of it. Each wave beneath her that pelted the ship reminded her of the impending nature of their predicament, her shrinking finances, and the greatness of the task before her. How would they manage?

"I am a sea raider. That is my occupation. I am not responsible for what befalls my freeloading passengers."

At this Joses spat into the sea, his disgust palpable.

Phoebe prayed they would not come to blows while more tears slipped from her eyes, which were fixed upon the nearing horizon. Soon they would be ashore. And then what?

CHAPTER TWENTY

Phoebe watched the land approach, as if in invitation. Though she wished it were the port near Rome that beckoned her, she reasoned that at least she could walk upon the earth, catch her breath, pray for perspective, and forge a new plan forward. Yes, perhaps God would reorchestrate something new. He was the One who made all things new, the God of the Resurrection.

Stavros continued to drop his sounding weight, measuring the sea's depth as they approached the port. It did not take long to reach their destination. Soon the sea raiders and their captain were taking the massive sail down, tying the ship to its new dock, and hollering all sorts of things that made little sense to Phoebe.

Joses kept himself busy with readying the boat to dock, so she stayed above, grateful for the scent of foliage and flowers wafting her way. She walked to the back of the ship, looking out at the sea for the longest time, while waning sunlight danced upon the water. It felt as though God chose to renew her resolve right there, instilling her with hope and determination—a welcome infusion of grace and strength. She tucked her hair beneath her palla, smoothed the wrinkles of her stola, and turned back toward the shoreline. She could see several of the men disembarking, carrying cargo upon their shoulders to be sold for the sake of Stavros. Such was the life of thieves who got away with their robbery.

She climbed down the ladder, and as she did, she called Trecia's name.

Once in their cramped quarters, she found Trecia's belongings gone. Did she miss her atop the ship? Must have passed in the commotion, she thought. Phoebe fished through her belongings, pulling back her cloak. There her beloved satchel sat. She pulled it up to place it upon her, but something felt odd. It did not have the same heft as it had before.

No!

She fumbled through the satchel, untying the leather strings. Relieved, she saw the parchment and fingered it. But wait. Only one. Not two. She pulled the room apart, searching with her hands. Did the other one slip out? On her hands and knees, she searched. She lit a torch, bringing it to every nook and cranny of the tiny room. Nothing.

Maybe Trecia had taken it as a way to bear half the burden. Yes, that had to be it.

She placed the single parchment back in the satchel, wrapped the cloak hastily around herself and ran through the ship's belly, torch in hand, Trecia's name upon her lips. But every small room where men had once been stood empty, save for the stench left behind. She opened every door, only to hear one voice in the distance—that of Regulus, still apparently chained. She ran to him. "Have you seen Trecia, my servant?" she asked.

The captain's eyes softened. "It has been reported to me that she has left, I am afraid. Dressed as a man, she ducked out, accompanied by Longinus."

"Are you sure?"

"As sure as these chains. You do not happen to have a key, do you?"

She shook her head, as she felt tears forming. This could not be. Had the girl not repented of Longinus's deception? Perhaps this was a ruse, a way to further their mission?

"I have seen Longinus do this before. He is not a good man, but I took him in as a favor to his parents. They had hoped the sea would tame him, make him honorable. But I am afraid the sea has no magical powers. It cannot transform a bad man into a good one. It does not morph wolves into sheep. I am sorry."

"What has he done with her?"

"That I do not know. But in the past, he has hoodwinked young girls, tricking them into thinking he fancies them, only to deliver them to a brothel ashore, pocketing much. I fear for your girl."

Dread climbed up her spine. "I am tasked to deliver these tent plans." She pointed to her satchel. "But one is missing."

"Longinus has a fascination for magic and potions. His is a bent toward darkness. I had heard him elicit details about the true nature of your parchments. That girl of yours convinced him that they had magical powers. That the words therein contained ancient wisdom."

She remembered the snippet of conversation in the corridor and suddenly understood everything, as if the sun broke through the clouds of her understanding. Theirs was no bent toward storytelling to pass the time; theirs was a secret tryst and a bent toward thievery. Phoebe ran from the protesting captain toward the ladder, then atop the ship. For a panicked moment, she saw no one, thinking Joses had abandoned ship as well, but then he appeared from behind the booming mast.

"You look afraid," he said. "Is everything all right?"

She crossed the short distance between them. "No. Trecia has left the ship."

"I did not see her."

"Captain Regulus, below, told me she disguised herself as one of the men and left." That was when she remembered the worst of the betrayal, as she carried it in her hands. She opened the satchel's mouth wide, showing Joses.

"Oh, this cannot be!"

"She has taken one of the parchments."

"Why did she take only one?"

"That I do not know. Perhaps she only wanted to half betray me."

Joses looked around. "She cannot be far. I will retrieve her."

"She is not an object to retrieve. And I fear she is in grave danger." Phoebe reached for Joses's forearm, as if to emphasize her point. "Longinus profits from delivering women to brothels."

"It is not safe for you ashore, as evening approaches," Joses said. "I will leave and find her. You stay here with the captain. He will protect you."

"How can he when he is in chains?"

"Follow me." Joses led her into the ship, toward the captain. "I know a thing or two about setting people free."

The captain's wrists were bloodied, as he had tried in Phoebe's absence to get free, and curses were on his mouth.

"Please, we are in the company of a woman," Joses said. "Hold still, and I will see if I can fix this." For what seemed like an hour, yet was truly only a few minutes, Joses used a narrow piece of metal to release Regulus from the chains.

"Why did you not do this earlier?" he snarled.

"Because Stavros ruled the ship, and you would not be enough of an uprising to unsettle him and his men. But you are free now. And I have a favor to ask of you."

"What is that?"

"Keep Phoebe safe while I look for Trecia."

"You will never find the girl, I am afraid."

"I have to try," Joses said. "She is important to Phoebe, and from what I have learned, she is in grave danger."

"Longinus is stealthy, young Joses. He is not easily tracked or caught. But may your searching bring favor, as I never thwart the hopes of one who has set me free."

"Thank you. And please protect Phoebe as night falls."

She felt as if she were a statue between them, being talked about but having no mouth to speak. All the shock from the last hour had yet to register fully within her. It was her mind that raced and chased and scurried about inside her like a mouse trapped in a box. What was happening here? "I will be fine," she finally mustered to say.

"Alone on a ship at night? I beg to differ," Regulus said. "But as long as you stay with me docked, we shall weather the night together." He turned to Joses. "Once you are off the boat, please stop in at the Rooster's Crow, and ask for Cornelius. Tell him I am in need of a new crew and a new cargo. He will understand. I cannot yet pay the crew, but there are many desperate men in need of work who will conscript themselves for me for future payment from the cargo. I know you must realize my predicament, having been stolen from in such a manner. Yours is not the only sad story."

"What will you haul?"

"That is up to Cornelius. But my hope is that it is a lucrative cargo. I now have creditors to pay, so it must carry twice its value. But that is not something we need to bother about right now."

Phoebe said, "Will you continue to Rome, or should we look for another way?"

"It is my hope that we will continue on as before, as I have important connections to make there. I am happy to take you there, but it will cost further."

Joses crossed his arms. "That is not our initial agreement."

"Sea raiding changes everything. As does desperation." He named his price while Phoebe did calculations in her head. It would take nearly all her money. Once they arrived in Rome, they would have little left. But that did not even matter if she did not possess the correct scroll. Either one gone would be a loss, but only one would be the ruination of the plan. "Before I agree, I must do something. Please wait here while I check something." She said this to both men then turned and headed toward her little cabin.

There, heart beating, she pulled the remaining parchment from its so-called secure place. She rubbed her hands along it, caressing it while she prayed. *Oh dear God, please be merciful to this journey.*

CHAPTER TWENTY-ONE

The wax reminded her of Paul, of their friendship, but the red pigment harkened her back to the story of Jesus, His death on that awful cross. She had never witnessed the spectacle of His demise, but she had seen a Roman crucifixion—not by intent but by accident. The agony she saw haunted her nightmares from that point forward. The bloodied man. The agonizing cries. The pulling up the ribcage to breathe, near suffocation as his arms weakened. When she had heard of Jesus and that He had endured such a disgraceful death, she wept. Yet He stayed there when He could have called upon legions of heavenly hosts to rescue Him. Love held Him to the tree, she knew. And the scroll before her, she hoped, told of this act. It detailed the Good News of the only good Man to ever live.

She nearly peeled the wax from the paper but hesitated, knowing the precious commodity that she held. Even paper itself was valuable—it held ideas, revolutions, dissolutions, declarations of marriage, court documents, philosophies—but none could compare to the pen of Paul's scribe. No, this letter superseded everything money could buy because it contained the words of life. Her heart pounding, she stopped.

She remembered the smudge.

Phoebe turned the scroll over, hoping for the barely visible ink smeared upon the scroll.

And there, like a miracle, was the smudge.

Yes!

In that elation, she remembered precisely how the letter began, remembered the tenor of Paul's voice as he dictated the letter to his scribe.

"Paul, a servant of Christ Jesus, called to be an apostle and set apart for the gospel of God—the gospel he promised beforehand through his prophets in the Holy Scriptures regarding his Son, who as to his earthly life was a descendant of David, and who through the Spirit of holiness was appointed the Son of God in power by his resurrection from the dead: Jesus Christ our Lord. Through him we received grace and apostleship to call all the Gentiles to the obedience that comes from faith for his name's sake."

She released the breath she had been holding in a *hallelujah*.

The letter was safe.

The mission toward Rome would continue.

She broke into tears, for nothing and everything there in the darkness of the dank cabin. She had told herself that she could not endure another betrayal. She had curated her life to stay safe from such agony by carefully choosing who she would let into her heart. As a deaconess, she helped those under her care, but there were times when her heart was not in it. This was known only to her, not to anyone else. She became adept at hiding her heart after Albus died, and she faced life without his parents, her parents, or the child that never was. She had made an internal declaration that no one could be trusted and that she would simply hang on until the resurrection of all things or until she breathed her last. And hang on, she did.

Hers was an internal declaration of independence. Oh, she would depend upon Jesus, yes. But she would not allow her heart to attach to another. But, as in life, all people need companionship, and she had let herself love and be loved by Trecia. Though she had declared that she could not withstand another betrayal, as she sat in the darkness, she realized her greatest fear had triumphed in Trecia's abandonment.

And yet?

She was not dead. She still breathed. She had not been utterly defeated. Hope remained, quite evidenced by the goodness of God, His shouldering of her tears, and the treasure she held in her hands.

Joses appeared at her doorway. "Is it there?"

She nodded, wiping tears from her face. "The letter is intact. Trecia took the wrong one—the map to Priscilla and Aquila's."

"But what if that was what she was after in the first place?" Joses asked.

"What do you mean?"

He sat next to her in the cramped quarters, and she wondered where the captain had ventured to, as she smelled Joses's sweat. Was she safe? Was she ever safe? She scooted away in the slightest movement, but he seemed to notice.

"I will not hurt you, Phoebe."

"Trecia said the same words."

"I can understand." He stood, placing distance between them. "What I meant was this. Remember when Paul warned constantly of false teachers? False prophets? He called them sheep among wolves. Which means they would appear like sheep, but inwardly they plotted to devour the church."

"But Trecia—she would not do such a thing. She was a sheep. I know it."

"Do you? Think back on your relationship. Can you be so sure?"

She traced their words through many nights, days, and conversations. Had she proclaimed Jesus as Lord? Everything seemed so jumbled in her head. "I hope she was."

"Hope is a powerful word, but we cannot fully rest our plans on the reliability of one human. Trecia may very well be deceived. She may be maliciously used by Longinus to uncover the whereabouts of the Roman church. This could be worse than stealing Paul's scroll. She may mean us harm. She may have delivered the killing orders to those who hate the church."

"I cannot think of Trecia this way," Phoebe said. "No, she has simply been deceived by Longinus. That is why there is one scroll. She peeked inside and delivered the lesser one to Longinus as a sign to us both—to trust that she was in too deep but still has a good heart."

Joses sighed. "I hope that is true, but I must act and pray as if it is not. Captain Regulus has chosen to stay aboard this evening as I send new crewmen his way. As you secured your doorway, though, when the sea raiders came, I beg you to do the same tonight. I do not trust any man at this moment. And I am loath to leave you here."

"The Lord Jesus is with me, just as He was with me through every trial. And He will be with you as well. Do you have a moment to pray before you disembark?"

He nodded.

She shared her worries, cares, bewilderments, and hopes with the One who shouldered her sins upon the tree. She asked for guidance, insight, and favor. She asked for Trecia's safety, blessings upon their journey, angelic intervention, and traveling mercies. She prayed for supernatural provision and protection. And with her amen, Joses too said a quiet amen, then left Phoebe as the darkness settled.

"God be with you," she said.

"It will be as you say," he replied as she secured her door for the long night.

CHAPTER TWENTY-TWO

Night was a terribly everlasting prospect when one was alone, lightly tossing to the shore's waves, particularly when a longing for land nearly overwhelmed all sense. But Phoebe stayed put, interceding for Joses, for Trecia, for the map. Through the slats above her, she spied the stars, remembering that the God who created all humankind named every star. None was outside His jurisdiction. He created the sun, the moon, the wood that created this ship, her heart, the grass of the field, and the flowers upon the hills, even her empty womb. All of it, His creation. Surely His heart was to show Himself kind and strong to the Roman believers. She tried to convince herself of that as she kept the scroll near. She would never leave it again until it was delivered into the hands of those who needed it.

As she prayed, she let her mind race to the worst possible outcomes. Trecia could be gone forever, the map in the hands of scoundrels, while Longinus continued to harm others. Joses could be injured or killed, leaving her alone in this room, this predicament. While those thoughts were unfruitful, they did help her think through what she could do. She could give Regulus her remaining funds, take the scroll to Rome by herself, and trust the Spirit to guide her through the twists and turns of unknown streets. Hadn't she heard of the crazy nature of church-persecutor Saul's encounter with the risen Jesus? And of Ananias who heard from God so clearly? He told him the specific house—Judas's home on Straight Street. Even while Ananias protested in fear, God reassured him. So he left everything, traveled to that place, found the man then named Saul, and placed his hands upon the blinded man, restoring his sight through the power of Jesus Christ. Yes, yes, God had led specifically. He would do so again, would He not?

A knock sounded at the door when dawn pressed through the inky night.

"It is Regulus."

"I have been instructed to keep my door barred."

"But I have food for you. Some fruit from shore. It is fresh. Would you like it?"

Her stomach said yes, but her resolve said maybe. Could she trust such a man? Was trust even important anymore, after so much betrayal? She remembered the caution of Joses but then thought of her strength, which had waned in the past few days. The rocking of the boat had caused much of her food to come up, and her heart felt weak. She pulled the wood from the door and opened it.

Regulus beckoned her. "Come eat it above deck. The sun is rising. It may bring some hope."

She wiped the evening from her eyes and followed the captain toward the beckoning sky. And he was right. The sun made its dawning appearance over the hills of Neapolis, pinking the sky and blazing orange. She remembered the psalm about weeping lasting for a night but joy shouting its insistence in the morning. She breathed in the day, sitting upon the rigging ropes, eating glorious figs perfectly ripe. The fruit tasted like love and friendship and joy all at once.

Captain Regulus laughed. "Be careful you don't eat too fast, or you'll lose it sure enough."

She wiped fruit juice from her chin. "Thank you for this. It means a lot to me."

"We are not all sea raiders, ma'am."

"Any word from Joses?"

"Afraid not." He pointed shoreward.

She followed his finger, her eyes landing on a small building with vines climbing up its walls. It made her long for home. "That is where Cornelius runs his inn. And that is where my next crew will come from. They are readying themselves now."

"Do you know when we will leave?"

He cleared his throat, then spit over the side of the ship. "Tomorrow night, as far as I can tell. We will be taking on new cargo soon."

"And how long until we reach Rome?"

"Should be just a day and a night once we set sail. We will hug the shoreline the whole time."

"Will that make it easier or harder to navigate?"

"Both."

He left her then to attend to parcels and packages of unknown contents, while she strained her eyes to see whether Joses would return before the sun went to bed. He disappointed her, which made her prayers increase along with her anxiety. She spent the evening locked in her room, while she heard the stomping of feet, the sound of carousing, and the smell of sour wine above her. All this added to her feeling of being utterly alone. She prayed until her eyes grew heavy, and the deep of night quieted the revelry from above. When she awoke the next day, she continued her bravery by unlocking her door, mounting the ladder, and milling about atop ship while men leered at her, and she feigned indifference.

Midday elevated her worry. Where was Joses? As the sun declared its descent, this worry wormed its way into her stomach, which had soured significantly. As the new crew readied the ship for sailing, she panicked inside. Should she disembark? Look for Joses? But then she would be all alone in a city she had never set foot in. But wouldn't that be her same fate if she stayed aboard and then went to Rome?

What was the last thing Joses had told her? That he would return, and that she should be safe. To be safe—would that mean leaving or staying?

Lord, what do You want me to do now? Should I stay? Leave? Please show me.

But no miraculous word came to her in her desperation, which confounded her greatly. She now wore the satchel across her chest as she had before, and its weight, though one parchment lighter, felt more burdensome, and the stares of the unfamiliar men unnerved her. Would this be the way she died? Would they have their way with her? She would have no protection, no way of defending herself. Fear grabbed at her as the sun sunk into the western sky over the sea. Though the light in oranges and rose pink fairly danced upon the waves, it brought no comfort. She would leave the ship. No other alternative existed. At least on land she could run away, but on a boat? Trapped.

She went beneath the deck, gathered her cloak and the last remaining figs, and climbed the ladder for the last time. She stumbled on the last rung, and a hand grabbed hers and steadied her. "Where are you going?"

Joses!

"You have returned! I nearly left the ship!"

He motioned for her to come to the back of the ship, saying nothing.

"Where is Trecia?" she whispered. "We cannot leave without her!"

"She has disappeared, I am afraid. I looked everywhere—even the brothels. I did hear from someone that she and Longinus appeared to be laughing as they took a road northward. I am afraid, Phoebe, that our worst fears about her are true. She is taking Longinus to the believers in Rome with no good intent."

"We must keep hope, Joses."

"Hope is reliant on actions, and hers are not noble."

"You have believed the worst of her," she said.

"And you have naively believed the best."

"But remember what Paul has taught us—that love hopes all things, believes all things."

"Yes, but it is also not mindless. You must face the possibility at least."

She shook her head, not knowing what to think.

"I have talked to Regulus," Joses said. "And he is bound to the port at Antium only, but that is fine. We will make our way from there without losing much time."

"This I already know. I have paid him for our passage."

"Everything?" Joses's voice sounded panicked.

"Nearly."

A long silence ensued while the first star pocked the night sky.

"We will be fine," he said finally.

"I do not know that to be true. But my attachments to this life feel less and less." With Trecia gone, what would she do? Whom would she share her heart with? Who would companion her long term? Certainly not Joses, as that would be improper. Certainly not any of these sailors.

"You must not give up. We are so close. We will see Priscilla and Aquila within the week, and then you will forget all of our troubles."

"I am not so sure. I have no idea where to go, where their tent-making shop lies."

"That is where our story makes an interesting twist." Joses smiled.

"Why?"

"Paul had also entrusted me with the directions, dear Phoebe. He made me repeat the way back to him several times. This is surely the providence of God, is it not?"

"Why did you not tell me earlier?"

"I was unsure I would return, so I kept the news quiet."

Phoebe's heart settled. "You know the way?"

"Absolutely. And I will take you there. We will deliver the scroll. You will read it and then set to getting it copied."

Relief. She let go of the anxiety that had built up like an ancient ruin. Joses knew the way. But in that moment, she wondered something. Would he truly help her?

"Are you all right?" Joses asked.

"I am not feeling well," she said. "I need rest."

"Very well," he said. "I will sleep above you as we have done in the past. If you need anything, just rap three times. I will answer you."

But as she pulled her woolen palla around her, as the satchel cut into her side, the loneliness of last night morphed from manageable to monsterlike. She could trust no one. When they finally disembarked in Rome, she would slip away, trusting only in the God who had brought her thus far.

CHAPTER TWENTY-THREE

When Antium beckoned them toward shore, Phoebe's plan was simple. Evade Joses while he finished settling the ship for dock, and, like Trecia, slip out among the others, hoping the Spirit would guide her to Rome and the Roman church. He had been enslaved once and knew how to make his way in the world. Surely he would be fine, and, she reasoned, he, of all people, would understand her abandonment. After all, this was the task entrusted to her, not him. She pulled her palla around her in the morning mist, being careful to always be on the opposite side of the ship of Joses.

When at last the ship moored at Antium's port, and ropes were flung ashore toward the dock, the riggings secured, she took note of a group of sailors laughing and telling stories. Just as Trecia did with Longinus, she thought. She wedged her way into their coarse conversation, feigning laughter, allowing their forward momentum to carry her down the plank, onto the dock, and toward land. The moment her feet touched the earth, she fought an urge to sink to her knees and kiss it. She had forgotten the steadfastness of solid dirt.

Once free of the group of men, she faced several pathways in front of her. Which one led toward Rome? She knew she had to veer northwest, but she was unsure which road took her there. And who was to know if the road crooked toward a turn in the distance? She had been familiar with the Roman road system in Cenchreae, but having never set foot upon this shore, the scene before her bewildered her, hastening her indecision. If she did not hurry to make a choice, Joses would catch up with her.

"Phoebe," came his voice from behind her.

She wheeled around, and there stood Joses, a look of pain on his face. She had expected anger, but not this. "I—"

Joses put his index finger to his mouth, shushing her as the wind picked up around them. "I am sure you did not mean to leave me behind," he whispered, his eyes weary.

"I am sorry."

He shook his head. "We have little time for banter. Words carry, and we have a task ahead of us. Besides, you are venturing down the wrong path."

She steadied herself, realizing there was nothing she could do to escape the inevitability of their companionship now. Besides, Paul had mandated that Joses protect her. And knowing the sovereignty of God, she had to surrender to this obvious change of plans. She remembered how Paul had intended to visit certain places on an itinerary only to be turned, stalled, thwarted, or prevented. In this case, God had pressed the two of them together. She finally spoke, "But these pathways? One of them must lead to Rome."

Joses laughed. "Alas, no." He pointed up the shoreline. "That is the way. You forget that I traveled with my master on many occasions. Even to Rome from this very port. Besides, I have Paul's voice echoing through me. We will make it, I promise."

"Promises are easily said but seldom kept," she said. Phoebe remembered the promises of her mother and father to walk alongside her in life, through wedding, children, their grand-children, and then into old age where she would have the priv-ilege of caring for them. Even now the ache of their dismissal remained, but a small shred of hope pulsed through her. One day, perhaps, they would come back to her, allowing their broken relationship to flourish again.

Joses walked toward the pathway toward Rome. "Stay near me, Phoebe. We are in constant danger, and I would hate for you to slip my notice as you unintentionally did just now."

She chastised herself for trying to tackle this task alone, in her own strength, without companionship. Trust was hard.

"Are you ready?"

She looked down at her feet, then thought of the history of Israel in the wilderness, a tale Paul often told—that the nation had survived forty years with the same shoes. Would hers—shoes meant for domestic duties only—survive the rocks beneath her feet? The past dictated that pain awaited her. She swallowed.

"This is the northward way toward Aricia, where we will hit the Appian Way, then venture into the great city."

With every step, Phoebe's heart grew heavier, the weight of Trecia's story weighing her conscience. "You looked every-where for Trecia, is that right?"

Joses sighed. "Yes, I have. That is why I almost missed the sea crossing. I asked questions in every place, but Longinus, though known well in those parts, had apparently perfected becoming a ghost, at least in that moment of time between disembarking and leaving the area."

Phoebe sighed. "All we can do is entrust her to God. His eye is upon her. He knows where she is. Our task is to forge ahead to Rome."

So forge they did, picking their way through the narrow path. Joses told her their trek to Aricia would take two long days of walking, followed by two more days once they ventured on the Appian Way. Joses mostly kept his voice to himself, preferring silence to banter for the first few hours as the sun rose to midday. They lunched in a grove of trees, a place that reminded Phoebe of Albus's healing and the beginning of their adventure with Jesus Christ. She broke their silence over figs and cheese they had purchased in the port by praying, thanking God for provision. She could no longer rely on her wealth to save her, this she knew. Perhaps this entire journey was not about the task—although it was important, to be sure—but to teach her that she had placed far too much reliance upon her stash of aureus instead of on the Messiah. Money had a convenient way of usurping her trust, providing for her. She had turned to it far too many times instead of first seeking the Lord. But here, under the trees as they neared Rome with their money nearly depleted, her prayer took on new meaning.

"Father, we thank You that You provide so beautifully. We acknowledge that You have brought us thus far. Please keep Your eyes upon Trecia. Protect her. She has been foolish, but You display Your power in our foolishness. So I entrust her to

You. And please guide us to the right place. Empower me to walk well. Protect my feet. And as we eat this meal, help us to remain grateful for all You have provided. If we finish this journey in hunger, I pray we would do it gladly, considering it a privilege to suffer for Your sake. So be it."

"Your prayers are beautiful," Joses said.

Phoebe felt a tear form in her eye. It escaped, then trailed down her cheek. She wiped it away.

"I have upset you, I am afraid." He ate a fig, chewing it slowly as if he were making it last.

"Yours are my Albus's words. He used to say such things to me before he—"

"No need to say more. I have lost many people in my life."

Though part of her was deeply weary from their journey, the tumults along the way, and the sheer amount of steps they must walk before they reached Rome, she felt the Spirit nudge her to tell Joses her story of salvation, as the grove of trees made the perfect illustration of the memory. "And you, Joses? What of you?"

"Mine is a complicated story, woven into my slavery narrative, I am afraid. I am unsure when I made haste to follow Jesus down that narrow path, as it had been part of my life under my Master's care. We were expected to follow Jesus."

Phoebe felt a familiar worry. Was his a real faith? Or a convenient one for the sake of harmony? "Did you resent that?"

"Yes, to be frank, I did. And when I found freedom—" But he said no more for a long time, the space of quiet growing longer.

She wanted to fill in that silence, but the Spirit kept her tongue stuck to the roof of her mouth. This was God's work, not hers. His promptings, not hers. His pathway, not her finagling.

He stood, while the sun shadowed him from behind. "When freedom came, I ran. Ran for my dear life. I resembled Longinus, slaking my appetites, chasing after everything and everyone. It was later, when I studied alongside Paul, that I found the writings of Solomon particularly poignant. He ran after everything the eyes could want, every task a body could do, every problem a mind could conceive. He had the means to do it all, and I had no means, but I still pursued it. Finally, like Solomon of old, I declared it all meaningless. For me it was like the climbing of infinite mountains, reaching the pinnacle, yet never celebrating because another summit loomed. The pursuit of everything exhausted my soul, swallowed my heart."

"I chased idols," she finally said, feeling the shame of those words. She shuddered to think how many times she had paid homage to gods and goddesses, figments of demonic deities that promised prosperity and a full womb but delivered despair and despondency.

"As did I, but they were not statues but things the world offered that never satisfied. I met Paul at my most desperate place," he said. "And that is when the real conversion took place. He explained to me the Good News of Jesus Christ, how he had persecuted the Way, how he stood smiling at the stoning of the martyr Stephen—gloating even, only to be knocked down by God and struck blind. When he recounted the story, I started shaking. I could not control my body or my fear. I felt I stood on holy ground, and that if I did not make a decision in that moment, I would forfeit my soul entirely." He motioned to a distant fork in the pathway ahead. "It was as if I stood there as you did this morning, seeing two differing paths. One led to life. One to death."

"So you chose life."

"No."

"What?"

"I ran. That had been my fallback my entire life. When things grew perplexing, I ran."

"Did Paul chase you?"

"No, but Timothy did."

She remembered the piousness and overall kindness of Timothy, Paul's companion. He was much younger than Paul. She could picture such a thing—Timothy in pursuit of Joses, which was really Jesus chasing his soul. "And what happened next?"

"He caught me. And everything that had ever happened in my life played before me in my memory. The pain. The worry. The regret. The enslavement. The fear. All of it pooled before me in my confession. Paul joined us as I spilled out my story. Together they told me what I needed to do—turn from my past ways toward God in repentance. When Paul laid his hand upon my shoulder after my lengthy confession, the Holy Spirit came powerfully upon me. I felt love like I had never experienced before. I sang, though I have a terrible voice. I wept out pain that had been lying dormant for years. And when it was all finished, I felt scrubbed, as if my heart had been washed in a clear stream. I finally understood the words my master had told me, about sins being as far as the east is from the west, about the joys of living in freedom. Mine was a complete transformation. And I only have Jesus to thank for such a story. Who would think a former slave could be so blessed by God? I am no one, but God has given me so much."

"Thank you for entrusting your story to me," Phoebe said. "It is a comfort to me to know we share the same affection for God. He has given so much. And now we are to rely on Him wholly for the remainder of this journey. We are nearly out of provisions."

He reached for her hand and pulled her to her feet. "In some ways, I view this predicament as providence. We are exercising faith with every step we make toward Rome."

"It is as you say," she said.

And they walked on in silence for many more miles.

CHAPTER TWENTY-FOUR

Smothered. That was what her dream told her. She could not breathe, could not move. In that frightening place between sleep and wakefulness, Phoebe struggled to understand what was happening, only to finally open her eyes in the darkness with a man's thick hand pressed over her nose and mouth.

"All of it!" he shouted.

She could see the stars above and a half moon, illuminating the man who smelled of creosote above her. Where was Joses? She tried to shake herself free, but her hands were bound somehow.

"All your aureus, even your denarii. Now!"

He let go of her mouth. She pulled in a breath, then used her exhale to scream for help. No one answered back.

Would this be the way she died? The Spirit replaced her palpable fear with something akin to boldness. "Where is my companion?" she demanded.

"He will be released to you once you comply." He reached toward the satchel.

"No," she heard herself say, as she bent away from his grasp.

"No?" The man's breath smelled like rotting flesh.

"No."

"I have the power to kill you."

"Whether you do or do not, I cannot say. But my God is with my companion and me, and He has secured our passage on an important mission. You will not take this satchel."

He grabbed her throat then, choking her. "I will have it and your breath!" He tugged the satchel easily from her grasp.

She tried to wrestle free, but she could not. Her own strength could not compare to the highwayman's. The stars above her danced as her mind struggled to keep the expanse above her steady, and she prayed desperately for breath. Life hovered toward death, and she felt her resolve move from fierce fighter to compliant capitulator. So this was how it ended? In utter defeat? Words undelivered. And yet...

Light broke through her narrowing vision—a light where no darkness dwelled, and its warmth felt like one thousand suns, yet never burning. Love lived there. All her insecurities and grief began fading in its warmth, and she felt her body grow limp beneath her. *Oh dear Jesus*, she prayed, *this is not such a struggle, death.*

The pull toward the light came at a whooshing speed, and she succumbed to it. Welcomed it. Wanted it with everything within her. Soon, the face of Jesus would fill her vision and all would be gloriously well.

A cold slap of water awakened her. Or was it a human slap? Her eyes adjusted to the darkness, blinking away the memory of love, though deeply longing for its insistence. She stood in the waning darkness, the trees where they had sheltered no longer there. She did not recognize this part of the trail. But one thing she did recognize: the satchel at her feet, unharmed. She grabbed it and pulled it to herself as tears wet her cheeks.

"You are all right?" It was the voice of Joses, pleading. His was not a tenor of confidence, but of panic, she knew.

Phoebe could not find her voice. She tried to speak, but her throat ached at the effort and her mouth felt dry and uncooperative. She nodded.

"They are gone."

"How?" she mouthed. No sound came out.

"I am not entirely sure myself." He reached for her hand, lifted her to standing. "You cannot speak?"

She coughed then, violent and unproductive.

Joses offered some water from the skin pouch slung around his neck. "Take this."

She drank hungrily as the cool water salved the sear of her throat. "Thank you," she finally said.

"We must keep walking until dawn. Keep moving. It is easier to thieve a sitting target than a moving one."

"I am tired."

Joses pointed down the pathway. "See here? We are descending at last."

"My feet." She looked down at her bleeding toes, the blood seeping through her shoes at the tips. Every step proved torturous.

"Here is what I have found," he said, beckoning her onward. "You will soon forget the pain if you keep walking. It is when you stop that the pain is insistent. When we reach the Appian Way, we will find a place to dunk your feet in cool water. It will bring much solace. But now? We must walk."

So walk they did, but neither spoke for many miles as the sun peeked over the horizon, welcoming the morning. It looked so pale and anemic compared to her vision that morning, that it did not cause any sort of celebration, just resignation for the task of walking step upon step. Each footfall became a labor. So she kept her perseverance by forcing herself to remember whole passages of the scroll she strapped across her chest. One passage roused her imagination.

And the Holy Spirit helps us in our weakness. For example, we don't know what God wants us to pray for. But the Holy Spirit prays for us with groanings that cannot be expressed in words.

Yes, this had been true in her life, particularly in her grief when she had no earthly words in her vocabulary to describe the pain within. Instead, she knelt by her empty bed then and cried out to the God of all comfort, choosing to trust Him, longing for relief from the pain. No words escaped her lips then, and none escaped now on the trail ahead of them. And yet the Spirit within her, who knew her better than she knew herself, understood every nuance of thought, worry, clay-footedness.

And the Father who knows all hearts knows what the Spirit is saying, for the Spirit pleads for us believers in harmony with God's own will.

She knew that at this moment as the light of day hit the sky's upper center, the Spirit pled for her and Joses. And Jesus? He sat at the right hand of God, interceding for His children, of which she was one. As she contemplated this beautiful truth, her mood shifted from anxiety to anticipation. There was nothing she could think of that God had not already thought of. He knew all. He carried all. He was the most intelligent Being in the world, she knew, and He would prepare a pathway for her. And whether she succeeded or failed mattered nothing in light of eternity. She was His child. Well loved. Carried. Living in the center of the powerful will of God. She smiled at the thought.

And we know that God causes everything to work together for the good of those who love God and are called according to his purpose for them.

Yes, this. God would take everything—even her past where idols replaced the Almighty—and use it to further His kingdom. She felt great solace in this, that this pathway she walked so painfully today had been ordained by the God who loved her implicitly. His purposes undergirded everything, even her lack of trust. And for that reason alone, she could persevere. She did not need to know the final earthly outcome; she could welcome it from afar, as a traveler anticipated the city he journeyed toward. In the New Heavens and the New Earth, all would make sense. The great weaver of stories would combine hers, Joses's, Albus's, and even Trecia's to bring glory to Himself and woo many to His side.

As she quietly recited this truth to herself, she thought of glory, which almost always meant weight and light together. She remembered her brush with death, the light that wooed, and the complete joy she felt in that moment. Glory was good. Not hers, but the One who inaugurated all glory.

Joses stopped, standing in the middle of the pathway, yellow fields to his left and right, gently swaying under the bluest sky. "We have no food," he said.

"True. But we have glory."

With that, he laughed, full throated and with such joy that she had to laugh herself.

Joses motioned to smooth boulders on the side of the path and indicated she should rest for a moment. "With this pace, we should reach the Appian Way before nightfall. But as we rest, I have much to tell you about what happened in the night."

"Please tell me," she said.

"There were two thieves, apparently. One had taken a rock and struck me upon the head. That is what I've been able to ascertain, as a rock lay nearby, and this." He pointed to the right side of his head where blood flowed through his hair.

"Oh no! Are you all right?"

"I think so. But only because of divine intervention. Do you remember anything?"

"Just waking up to choking, and my hands bound."

"But no other memory?"

"No. How did we escape?"

"A warrior of a man intervened."

"What?"

"I don't know who he was, but he apparently pulled me to my feet, told me all would be well, then struck the two men with one blow. He took your hand and mine, and led us through the darkness a few hundred feet."

"I have no memory of that."

"When does your memory return?" he asked.

"Standing in a new place with the satchel at my feet, hearing your voice."

"I have heard of something similar—with Philip," Joses said. "He had been preaching the Good News to an Ethiopian eunuch, baptized the man, then found himself miles away in Azotus. Plucked by the Almighty! Imagine that!"

"I have often thought those stories to be fit for folks like the apostle Paul, not for regular people like you and me."

"It is hard to imagine, but as I look back on my life," Joses added, "I have seen supernatural occurrences—mostly evil. It was only in my conversion that I began to see light pierce through those dark battles. Phoebe, I believe we have encountered an angel."

Phoebe pulled in a breath. She had heard stories of interventions like these, but surely she was not worthy of an encounter of this sort. "I do not know what to say."

"I suppose we say very little except to express our worship to God who is obviously watching over us. I only wish the thieves had not taken our money. I am hungry."

"I am too," she said. Her stomach growled back as the exclamation at the end of her quiet declaration. Truth be told, it was more like a quiet desperation. Though fasting had been an integral part of her spiritual disciplines, the past practice did not make the present circumstances any easier, especially when forced upon someone through thievery.

Still, they plodded forward. She did find that her feet seemed to forget their pain. As the light changed from late midday to dusk, Joses stopped, then whistled.

"What is it?"

He pointed to a fig tree at their right. "I believe the good Lord has provided supper."

"But what if it belongs to someone?"

He looked around. "I see no one. Remember the words of Jesus? That God feeds and clothes the birds of the air? Well, we are His valued treasures, His 'birds' in need of food. And this tree is ripened and welcoming. I say we partake."

They plucked several ripened fruits from the tree, placing them carefully in Joses's satchel. Figs bruised easily, but they tasted like heaven, she knew. Her mouth watered at the gathering. Finally, they sat beneath the tree, wholly in need of rest and shade. Phoebe could feel perspiration wet her back. "How much longer until we reach the Appian Way?"

"Should just be two more hours of walking." He pointed in the distance. "See that grove of tall trees on the periphery? Just over there."

She took her palla and smoothed it onto the ground beneath the tree. They sat there while she said a prayer. "Oh dear Father, Lord of all creation, we thank You honestly and earnestly for Your surprising provision today—both for these figs, and the intervention of the large man. Was it an angel? We do not know, but we remain utterly grateful. Please bless this food to our bodies as we seek to travel longer. Amen."

"Amen." Joses plopped a fig in his mouth and smiled. Purple juice trailed from the corner of his lips to his chin, but he did not choose to wipe it clean with his hand. Instead, he licked the juices.

Phoebe laughed.

When she ate her figs, she told her stomach to accept them. All the worry she had encountered on this trip had soured her insides, so she hoped the figs would stay put. Thankfully, they went down smoothly, and she didn't revisit them later.

The last two hours of walking felt both unnerving and joyful—if those two emotions could exist simultaneously. Unnerving because the time passed slowly, and the hillside never seemed to come near. Joyful because Joses filled their time with songs from his youth—words and lyrics she did not know. But by the end of their trek, they became as familiar as a worn tunic. They sang as they walked to the Appian Way, but when they met the road, Phoebe was unimpressed. She had thought it would be a bastion of civilization, with merchants and commerce, but instead, the way was simply a rock-pocked road, smoothed over, Joses said, with lava stones.

"At least it is flat," he said, smiling. "From here, it is two days' walk to Rome. We need to find shelter for the night. A storm seems to be making its way from the coast." With that he looked toward the sunset, his rough hands over his eyes.

Phoebe followed his gaze. The sun rather dazzled the water of the great sea in hues of purple and vermillion, but above that splendor loomed a darkening gray mass of clouds. Lightning flashed in the distance, and echoing thunder answered back. Sheltering beneath a tree would not be advisable. If only they could find a home or a barn. She remembered the stories of Jesus having no formal place to be born, being relegated to a barn for His birth. She would welcome such a provision.

Joses laughed as the thunder continued. "We will be well! I do know a person nearby."

"You are just now remembering this? Why did you not relieve my worries earlier?"

"I am not entirely sure he is nearby—only by rumors, but his name is Ennius, and he too is a tentmaker." Joses ran toward a group of men by a well. He motioned with his hands, laughed a few times, and pointed back to her.

In that place, she felt vulnerable. She could not defend herself, nor could she offer money as a bribe if they got in trouble. For so long she had prided herself on taking care of herself, though a widow. The church in Cenchreae had relied heavily on her resources, and Paul had come to respect her for not only her financial remuneration, but also her thoughts, her heart, her dedication to all things related to Jesus Christ and the Gospel. She loved being needed. She needed that. And perhaps her identity had woven itself intrinsically to this idea. *No child,* she heard the Spirit say, *whether you are needed or in need, you are worthy. Now watch how I take care of My children. I am a good Father. Rest in Me, Phoebe.*

Joses returned to her, smiling. "Yes, Ennius lives less than an hour from here, but the storm is fast moving. We must race to get there. Are you up for running?"

"Do I have any choice?"

"No, I am afraid not."

She wrapped her palla over her head, gathered up her skirt, pulled up her stola, then her tunic, and tried to keep up with Joses's stride. They must have looked like an odd pair—a harried man and woman running to beat the rain. But she didn't care. She had heard rumors of lightning strikes, how they rendered a person shocked, then dead. Behind her the rumble of thunder gathered a faster beat. She told herself not to fret, but with each flash and answering boom, her mind feared the worst.

"Hurry," Joses said.

"I am doing my best," she said, breathless. Fat raindrops splattered upon her, wetting her palla and saturating her scalp. Then more, followed by a deluge of Noachian proportions. Her feet slipped on the rock roadway beneath her. She prayed she would not tumble to the earth. And she prayed even more that the document in her satchel would stay dry and unaffected. Yes, she had memorized portions of it, but how would she ever know for sure that she got it right if the ink smeared? This single thought propelled her forward. Surely they would find shelter soon.

Joses jutted right, and Phoebe followed. There stood a small cabin made of rock and earth. He rapped on the door with a fierceness that made her both proud and a little fearful. "Please," he said. "We are friends of Priscilla and Aquila." For what seemed like several minutes, nothing happened, no voice answering, no stirring from within. Surely they had the wrong place.

But precisely at that moment of her despair, the door opened. There a man stood, hair gray and wild, a smile creasing his face. "I am Ennius," he said. "Come in. You will catch a consumptive disease in this storm. Hurry!" He ushered them into his dry and cozy home—just a small room heated by a rock fireplace, crackling and spitting sparks into the room's center.

Joses pulled his cloak from his head. "I am Joses, and this is Phoebe."

"It is my pleasure. I have heard stories of people having the privilege of hosting angels in situations like these. Tell me, are you angels?"

Joses laughed. "No, we are of the same skin and breath as you."

Ennius pointed to a table where four roughly hewn chairs circled it. "Please sit."

Phoebe too removed her palla, now saturated.

"Here." Ennius took her palla and Joses's tunic and laid them out by the fire. "This will dry them by morning." He looked toward the ceiling and said, "Thank You, Father, for Your provision!" He smiled and then stirred something that smelled like heaven in the black pot over the fireplace. He looked at Phoebe. "The Good Lord told me that I would be having guests and that it would need to be hearty, whatever it was I prepared. So I made this stew from the last bit of lamb I had, threw in a few vegetables from my garden, prayed, and longed to eat it! But no!" With this he flourished with his hands. "No! God told me to wait. To be honest, I did not want to wait. I am an impatient man. But I have found in my life that when one argues with the Almighty, one loses the argument."

"I am grateful for provision," Phoebe said. "But I am afraid I have nothing to offer you for your hospitality."

Ennius sat opposite her at the table where a single candle lit his weatherworn face, as the thunder grumbled above them and the lightning illuminated the outdoor air. "Stories are my payment. Nothing more. You give me stories, and I feed you. Will that work?"

"Yes." She smiled.

"You two married?" With this question he smiled again and laughed. "I have never been married. Always wanted to be. But God had different plans. And now I serve Him in this strange outpost. Every day, I tell you, is an adventure, conjured up by God Himself. Today you two are my adventure! I am nearly bursting with joy at the thought of it all!"

"We are grateful," Joses said. "We are not married. Phoebe is a widow and a deacon from the church in Cenchreae. I am a former slave tasked with protecting her. Together, we carry words from the apostle Paul to the believers in Rome."

Ennius clapped his hands together. "What a story! What a privilege!"

"Well, the story is not yet completed," Phoebe said.

"Let us eat first, then share." Ennius fussed around them, setting the table and bringing the lamb stew to them. He poured dollops of the meaty broth into large bowls and then flanked each with a slice of rough-cut bread.

Butter sat gloriously in the table's center, practically begging to meet the bread. Phoebe obliged the request, slathering butter upon the heavenly piece. When she tasted it, she nearly groaned with joy. It had been a long time since she had bread—at least fresh, leavened bread like this. She dunked her slice into the stew, took a bite, and smiled. "This is heavenly, Ennius. You are a tremendous cook. Thank you."

He sat back, not eating, his arms crossed over his chest. His smile wrinkled his entire face and seemed to make his eyes dance in the candlelight. "I have no greater joy than to serve the body of Christ in such a way. You are my blessings, Phoebe and Joses."

She ate until fully satisfied, and Joses followed—all while Ennius told stories of other visitors along the Appian Way—some Christ followers, some pagan, all chock full of intrigue, the mundane, and most of all, humor. He offered them cozy pallets on the floor near the fireplace, Joses beneath the table, and her on its other side. Though she should have felt apprehension, the Spirit warmed her to sleep, and peace quickly overtook her.

CHAPTER TWENTY-FIVE

With the morning came the sun, gloriously alive as it rose in the hillside behind Ennius's cabin. Phoebe spent an hour or so in prayer in the dewy grass as the light changed from dusky gray to bright blue. Ennius filled them with a hearty morning meal and prepared to send them on their way with a robust prayer, a satchel of provisions, and a warning.

"Rome is not a friendly place for a woman," he cautioned. "Stay near her." This he directed at Joses, and Joses nodded his compliance.

The care in Ennius's voice stirred that familiar longing in Phoebe, to be loved again by her earthly father, to be cherished and delighted in as her mother had done for so many years. She had heard people say that once they met Jesus, His Body became their family. And in the light of another long day they faced, her belief in such a truth was strengthened. This man acted as a father, an uncle, a patron, a friend. He had, no doubt, given the last of his provisions so they could have a successful journey. His sacrifice nearly made her weep.

Ennius tenderly touched her upper arms, his eyes brighter in the morning dawn. "The apostle Paul has entrusted you with treasure, genuine gold, dear Phoebe. But I am looking at the real treasure. It is you. You have much to offer us all, much to add to the glorious Body of Christ. You do not realize this yet, and your name may never grace the tomes of history, but be assured—God sees you. He will be with you. And He will lead you in this journey."

She sputtered a thank-you.

He kissed each tear-stained cheek. "Now be gone, the two of you. There are people in need of this treasure."

Though her feet ached and her lower back felt sore from her time on the floor, the morning air was fresh, and it revived her. She hadn't realized that Ennius was just what she needed in that very moment to continue. She needed the affection of a father, the kind words of a mentor, the provision of a friend.

They walked under a cloudy sky that day, the sun dipping in and out of the white puffy expanse. Joses pointed out a lavender field, and they plucked a few stalks. Phoebe pressed the tiny purple flowers between her hands, releasing their heady scent. Memories of dear Trecia wafted back in, almost violently. Strange how a scent could usher in such joy and despair all at once. She prayed for Trecia, hoping upon hope that she found her way back to truth, to life. She remembered the crushing of God in her own life, even over the past few weeks, and how He had used that crushing to better her. As she looked back over her life, she noticed the trend. When life felt easy, growth stalled. When difficulties arose, thriving ensued. She had prayed a few weeks prior to this task that God would grow her in new ways. She expected that growth to come from further learning or serving where God planted her. But He had other plans for her, pushing her away from comfort and what had become easy into the scary unknown. And in that place, her faith had flexed its wavering muscles, found its grit, and grew despite the trials.

Joses seemed almost mute on this day. His face grew more troubled the closer they neared Rome. She tried to pry from him the reason for his seeming sadness, but his responses came out curt, tense. So to pass the time, and to forget the blisters upon blisters her feet boasted, she played a game with herself. Their way was hilly, with olive groves scattered here and there, while conical cypress trees lined the pathways to great estates. Each hill, she decided, represented a year of her life. So with each hill, she traced the handiwork of God in that year. Year one, she thanked Him for saving her from an unknown childhood disease where she apparently broke into a long-standing rash, accompanied by fever. Mother had bathed her in salt water, dotted with lavender, in hopes to quell the itch. She had paid homage to a local deity, and the rash subsided. Phoebe chose today to praise God for His clear intervention in saving her life, despite her parents' superstitions.

Year five she fell from a tree, nearly twelve feet in the air, landing crudely on her left arm, dislocating the shoulder so her arm hung limp. It just so happened that a local handyman had been working on their home at the time, and he knew the art of putting a limb back in its place—another picture of God's grace.

She recounted several times of divine intervention where she should have been harmed but had not. And she noted her deep longing throughout her childhood to understand the world. This hunger drove her into the country, to inspect ants as they paraded in lines, to listen to the birds call to each other, each in its own particular warble. She lay on her back in summertime when chores were finished and watched the clouds change into shapes of animals and flowers above her.

At age thirteen, on one such recline, she spoke the words out loud, away from the ears of her parents. "Whoever You are who made all this, I want to know You." It had been a prayer, a pleading, an inquiry. And now, as she walked the Appian Way toward an uncertain future, she saw the hand of God as He spent the next several years wooing her to Himself. What a beautiful legacy she had! And how tenderly He loved her, even in her rebellion and ignorance.

When she reached yet another hill and recounted the day God saved her, she could feel the tears form in her eyes. That day marked the beginning of her new life but the decided end to her other. God had drawn a line in the sand before Jesus and after Jesus. And although it still pained her to know that her family felt her an enemy, knowing Jesus was far better.

A few more hills and she arrived to where she stood today as dusk fell upon a hushed afternoon. Mosquitoes buzzed nearby in lazy circles over a lifeless pond. She pulled in another breath. Tomorrow evening they would reach Rome, and everything would change again. But God had proven Himself utterly faithful.

Joses stopped. "It looks to be a pleasant evening. Up there is a large tree we can sup under then sleep. I will gather some wood for a fire."

She wanted to say, "Thank you for finally talking," but she kept quiet. A strange reticence had overtaken him, shadowing his face. She prayed that the Lord would settle his mood by tomorrow with the new dawn. But she feared Joses would keep silent for the rest of their journey.

CHAPTER TWENTY-SIX

The whirring of locusts, the sound of birds chirping, the rustling of yellowing grasses—these woke her up. Phoebe tried to quell her fear. After all, this would be the day they would reach their destination after so many tumults. "Did you sleep well, Joses?"

He simply nodded then grunted through their morning as they paced toward Rome. Alarm blossomed in her the quieter he became. She had naively believed her parents would meet Jesus when she shared Him with them, but, instead, they disowned her. She had placed her rightful trust in Trecia, who had earned it over the years, and had been betrayed and abandoned. She had wavered in her faith in Joses, at times seeing brilliance of character, with compassion and honesty undergirding him, but at others, glowering like today. His was a countenance of chaos, a man of kindness for a long duration but punctuated by short bouts of annoyance. Though, in today's case, the bout had maintained. Did he actually know the way to Priscilla and Aquila's? Was his silence an indication of plotting like Longinus, of delivering her over to those who would harm her?

She tried to focus on Paul, his earnest face, his urgent request. If she thought of him and the words he wrote that she cradled next to her body, she would endure Joses's silence with grace. If she remembered the faithfulness of God, she felt peace. But the ongoing silence picked at her, as a mosquito hones in on its victim, stinging, stinging, stinging until it had its fill of blood.

As they ate the remnants of Ennius's provisions at the noon hour, she could stand it no longer. "Tonight we will be in Rome, but you are far away, I fear."

He shook his head and rubbed his chin. "I will take you to the destination, but then I will leave as quickly as I came."

"Why?"

"I cannot say." His voice was tinged with the deepest sadness—or was it regret?

"I deserve to know," she said.

"I am unsure if that is wise." He ate his last fig, wiped his mouth with the arm of his tunic, and stood. He paced beneath the tree where they supped.

"What is it, Joses?"

"I am wrestling with God."

"That is a dangerous task, I fear. How is your hip?"

His stern face bore a flash of a smile. "I am no Jacob."

"Well, good, because the last thing we need on this trek is you with a hip out of socket. We are still hours away." She tried to keep her banter lighthearted, hoping he would catch it.

Joses sighed. "All will be well, right?"

She packed up their things then ventured back to the Appian Way, where further foot torture awaited. "Yes, I believe so. But I fear for you."

"Why?"

"You are holding something inside that may prove to be our downfall. Do not ask me how I know this. It is just a sense I have from the Spirit. And it has unsettled me. Please do not keep a secret for long. Wrestle if you must, but remember that truth trumps darkness, and honesty brings light. The enemy wants to torture us in the darkness. He wants nothing better than to steal, kill, and destroy, and he begins this descent by isolating God's children. Today you have lived apart from me, at least in your imagination. But I am right here. I need you."

"Thank you for saying that. I am not accustomed to being needed in such a way. As to your inklings—some words are better left unspoken."

They passed another hill, and this time Phoebe tried in vain to find God's faithfulness in the moment but could not. The bleakness of Joses's mood permeated even the afternoon birdsongs. They sang. She dreaded. They chirped. She worried. They made melodies. She ruminated.

Joses said nothing as they approached the outskirts of Rome. She could tell they were nearing the great city by the increase in homes and businesses dotting the landscape at greater frequency.

Finally, throwing aside decorum, she grabbed his arm to stop him.

"What?" he asked, his eyes wet.

"Tell me. What is it that bothers you? And why now? I will go no farther until you do."

"Do not hold the mission hostage on account of me. I will be fine. I have always been fine."

"That is not what you said earlier."

He walked forward.

She stood in place like a marble statue in a temple.

He turned.

She placed her hands on her hips and shook her head no.

He let out the longest breath of their journey. "I will tell you," he said. "But we must walk as I do. I do not want to see your face as I share."

For hundreds of painful footfalls, he said nothing. The day warmed while they passed a few hawkers selling wares—tapestries, ripened fruit, painted stones. He nodded to each but continued his vigil of wordlessness.

On one particularly taxing hill, he spoke. "You will no longer want me as a companion," he said. "So I will tell it plainly."

Such alarm tinged his voice that she almost reached out to touch his arm, but she refrained. His was a pain that seemed to not want pity, and certainly touching him would not be proper. Still, her heart ached at the tension she saw in his shoulders.

"I am still a slave," he said.

What?

She told herself to not react to his words, told herself to calm down. But internally? What was she to do? She had been taking a journey with what—an escaped slave?

"Most of everything I told you was true."

"*Most* is not the same as *all,*" she said, controlling her fear.

"I know. And I am sorry. Truly sorry. My story has been eating at me this entire journey, but it roars at me from within the closer we come to Rome." He wrung his hands as he continued. "My master had always been a pragmatic man, one prone to mathematics and numbers. His is a business whose balance sheet runs smoothly on the backs of others. It is how he made his fortune. After he had me pierced, I began to despair. Hope returned when he met Jesus Christ. This would be my way out. I could reason with him, remind him of what happened to me."

"Because you have this story, I am assuming he did not hear you."

"You are correct," he said. "On the contrary, he asserted his right to own me for the rest of my life, citing the piercing as proof of his rightness. For several weeks I despaired. My small community of believers on the Macedonian estate comforted me. One of them, a wise old man whose eyesight was dimming, told me to continue to serve with gladness, then pray for an opportunity to mention Zaccheus."

"Why Zaccheus?" Her feet continued their less-than-silent protests as they continued walking toward Rome.

"His story brought me much comfort. I prayed through what I knew of that story—of a tax collector who climbed a tree, who welcomed Jesus into his home, all those notorious sinners surrounding Him. Oh the audacity! I would have much liked to be a bee buzzing about that room. Imagine the conversation!"

"Yes, but what precisely made the old man mention him?"

Joses shook his head, as if ridding himself of some dark memory. "It was a fool's errand, these prayers I prayed. When the time was right, I expected to share the story of Zaccheus, how he repented of everything—all the stealing, the greed, the preference of mammon to man. I thought the master would appreciate my retelling of the story, particularly the repentance part—that if the tax collector had wronged anyone, he would pay them back plus more. Jesus rewarded him with words about true salvation coming to Zaccheus. His reward would be great in the life to come."

"The time to tell the story," Phoebe said. "It must have come?"

"Yes. He invited his servants to a feast, much like the Zaccheus feast, I imagined. He said he had made a spiritual decision and that we would want to hear it. He smiled at us all, lifted his cup in salute, cleared his throat, and said five words that sunk my heart."

"What did he say?" Phoebe noticed the sameness of Joses's expression, but the corners of his eyes moistened.

"'We are now a church.' That is what he said. He saw it as his Christian duty to form us into a congregation. He would allow us time off to sing a hymn, share a story, pray for one another. But he made no mention of setting us free. Some of us had been serving him many stretches of seven years. Seven, then seven more, then multiples of seven. I felt the air in his quarters leave the room. I dared not make eye contact with my fellow slaves. We would all cry out if we did such a thing. My master's *religion* had not transformed his heart. Rather, it had cemented his resolve to enslave men and secure his future. I lost all heart, Phoebe."

"But you are here. And now you walk beside me. Are they not chasing you?"

"I would assume so. And now I have broken your trust in the meantime."

"This is true."

He said nothing but kept walking. Then, "Even the apostle Paul did not know of my arrangement. Otherwise he would not have sent me to companion you on this journey."

They crested the hill before them, the sun beginning its descent toward the great sea to their left, while the world was bathed in gray to their right. Below them stretched Rome. Phoebe stopped. "There she is."

"Yes, in her splendor."

Phoebe suddenly felt fear overtake her anger over Joses's lies and treachery. "But you cannot accompany me."

"I will still complete our mission, come what may."

"You do not have to," she said, but she did not mean her words. Even if he told her the directions to Priscilla and Aquila's she did not trust her own sense of direction to locate them. The weight of her satchel felt as heavy as a large dog.

"I made a promise."

"By leaving, you broke a promise to your master."

"I did," he said, as they descended the hill toward Rome. "This has been eating at me the entire trip, and even before that if I am honest. I had an opportunity to be completely truthful with Paul, but I chose not to be. He looked me in the eyes and asked if I had anything I would like to share with him, but I said no. I had hoped that simply putting the past behind me and choosing a new life would erase my escape. But the farther the ship brought me from Macedonia, the more restless my heart became, and the reality of my state weighed upon me."

"What changed your mind? Why are you telling me?"

"I have watched you endure hardship with grace. I have listened to your stories of loss, and yet you persevered, even when the outcome was uncertain. Your faithfulness served as God's reminder that I must do the same—to live truthfully and accept the consequences of my fleeing."

Phoebe worried then. What would happen to Joses, a man she had grown to rely on? Would he be imprisoned? Would he serve the rest of his life as a slave? "What are you going to do?"

"When I finish helping you, I will return to Macedonia and turn myself in."

They continued their descent as the air cooled and birds chirped goodbye to the day.

"Do you not want to know how I left?"

She wanted to admit her curiosity but thought it wrong. So she kept quiet as their leather soles slapped the black road beneath them.

"Four nights after his church declaration," he said, "I approached my blind friend to tell him my intentions. I expected him to talk me out of my plan. But he simply told me that freedom from bondage is always the greater good. I did not know what he meant by that, but I chose to believe he endorsed my leaving. What I did not realize until later, when I heard the news, was that he was most likely referring to his own emancipation. The day I left was the day his soul rose to God. In my panicked state of living on the run, particularly in the rush of the newness of it all, I envied him. He lived finally free from all constraints. Me? By situation, I was free, but in my heart, I lived in torment from guilt and fear of being found out. In order to find solace, I ran. Then ran some more. Then kept fleeing, leaving Macedonia until I met Paul in Cenchreae. He did not know my story, though I constantly feared the Holy Spirit would tell him."

Rome was so near, she could nearly touch the outskirts, but she slowed her pace to hear the story. Phoebe feared that when he finished, he would leave her. Best to abbreviate her footfalls.

"But nothing of the sort happened. Instead, Paul befriended me, taught me a trade, and poured his life into mine. I became his disciple—he my rabbi of sorts, and me the student, content to follow behind him, in the dust of his footfalls and genius. When I was in his presence, my fears ceased. But at night? The fears returned. I would be found out as a slave on the run. And my life of freedom would end much worse than it began."

"I don't know what to say," Phoebe responded.

"There is not much to say, I would imagine. You have been forsaken by your parents, bereft of your spouse, betrayed by your close friend, and the man walking beside you is a criminal. There is no tie between us that you cannot sever, and I would expect nothing less."

"Only Jesus is reliable."

"That is true. I have experienced His trustworthiness for many years. It has sustained me through dark nights and tumults."

"I struggle to trust you," she said. "But I can choose to rely on the Spirit who is the same One who shares my heart. Do you promise to stay with me? To help me complete our mission together?"

"I do not want to put you in danger. My master is a powerful man with tentacles reaching throughout the Mediterranean."

"But you have already put me in this danger, the moment you acquiesced to Paul's request."

"It is as you say. I am deeply sorry. I pray you can find forgiveness in your heart for my foolish recklessness—that I put you in possible danger because of my own fear. I do not deserve such pardon, but I do seek it."

Forgiveness had never been easy for her. Phoebe had never been one to run joyfully toward pardon—that had been Trecia's kindhearted tendency, not hers. No, she thought things over, rolled them around in her mind trying to make sense of betrayal. And no matter how many angles she looked at an issue from, this kind of stepping away never made sense to her. But as they walked in silence toward an unknown outcome, Phoebe realized that with Trecia, she had not considered life from her perspective. Knowing Joses as she had these past few weeks, she understood that every human being had a right to be free of ownership. Perhaps Trecia's escape was less about her betrayal and more about her longing to live life without shackles of indentured obedience. If Phoebe had a pond to gaze into in that moment, she would have to admit that she too bore guilt. "I will consider it," she finally said.

Joses exhaled. "That is all I can ask."

As the day finished its last hallelujah, they discussed where to go next. His decision to stay with her, coupled with her decision to walk alongside him, became an unspoken covenant. Their mission superseded everything else.

Joses pointed northwest. "Once the Appian Way intersects the outskirts of Rome, we will veer right, flanking the city toward the north. But be alert. Stay near me. I am saddened that we arrive at nightfall. Hopefully we will find merchants selling torches so we can light our way."

"Before we go any farther," Phoebe said. "I feel compelled to pray."

Joses nodded.

They stepped away from the road. Joses began, "Father in heaven, thank You for the grace of Phoebe not to expel me. And thank You for giving me the courage to finally come clean. As You did with King David, You have suddenly and beautifully cleansed my heart, and I am light again. This is Your doing. We both choose to trust You, even as we tremble. So be it."

"Amen," Phoebe said. "And dear God, I ask for Your help in learning to move on after a broken heart. It is hard for me to voice it here under the canopy of the sky You made, but I have let bitterness inform me more than blessing. It is a privilege to suffer for Your sake. It is a privilege to bring the words of life to those in desperate need. Cleanse me from any pride, and lead us in the way everlasting. We trust You for this final part of our pilgrimage. Please guide us. Be with us. Amen."

Joses's amen to her prayer ended their heavenly discourse and inaugurated their descent into the belly of Rome.

CHAPTER TWENTY-SEVEN

Phoebe pulled her wool palla around herself as stars pricked the night sky. They were near, Joses told her, but her feet did not feel glad. No, they rebelled, begging her to stop their relentless pace. "Are you sure we are near? I need to rest."

Joses said nothing. Glowering had replaced the lightness of their prayer as they walked up and down crooked streets. "I thought it was here," he finally said. He pointed to a narrow walkway that led to a nondescript doorstep, no torch illuminating the way. "But I cannot be sure."

She resisted raising her voice, knowing that ears and eyes could hear and see them. Christ followers were not the most welcomed of people in this tangle of confusing streets—most without names—and with the sun gone from guiding them happily, everything seemed dour and frightening to her. Shadows leapt at her. She startled at every turn, but now standing and facing the darkened corridor, with her feet spent several *stadia* ago, Phoebe nearly cried. "I do not care if you are sure or not. We must find a place to settle. Perhaps we will be met with favor."

Joses rubbed his eyes, shaking his head. "We have come so far," he whispered, which added to the anxiety within. "I must be entirely sure."

She let go of fear in lieu of exasperation then, not caring a whit about her voice level. "Does trust mean knowing everything before you take the next step, Joses? Or does it mean going forward in the mystery? I opt for the latter. Is that not what I did with you? Had I known your predicament and crime prior to leaving, I would not have ventured forward. You were the unknown. Had I known Trecia's slippery ways, I would have left her behind. But here we stand in the great city of Rome, immobilized—me with bleeding feet and you with trepidation. I say we knock."

He said nothing, but walked toward the doorway. No sign above it indicated a tent-making enterprise. No one milled about in front of the place, not even in the outer walkway. So he knocked, three heavy raps.

And they waited.

He knocked again. "Must not be here. Or perhaps I have misunderstood Paul's directions."

An almost unperceived small door opened. An eye lit by candle looked directly at Joses, while Phoebe stayed behind him. "What is the second feeding miracle?" came the voice behind the door.

"Excuse me?"

"The number of people He fed the second time."

Joses turned to Phoebe. "What is this? What do you think they mean?"

"Jesus fed the five thousand with five loaves and two fish. The second time, I believe it was four thousand. Perhaps that is what they are asking?"

"Four thousand," Joses said.

The tiny door shut with an equally tiny reverberation on its hinges. And then nothing. Phoebe could hear Joses breathing. She smelled the acrid odor of burning garbage, heard the pining of a pair of doves singing to the night. Everything slowed down in the wait.

Joses turned. "We have come to the wrong place. We will need to leave the city and stay the night in the country, for our safety's sake."

But then the door swung wide open, light emanating from inside. "I am Priscilla," came the voice attached to the beautiful eye. "Come in."

Phoebe had not realized she had been holding in a breath for their entire journey, and all at once in the warmth of the entryway, she fell to her knees. Tears poured from her as Joses placed his hand upon her head. They had found the place, the people, the church. After so much toil, fear, abandonment, and twists and turns.

Priscilla, wearing a blue-and-white stola and a stunning white palla, lifted Phoebe to her feet. "Tell me your name," she said, her voice melodic and oozing sincerity.

"I am Phoebe of Cenchreae," she said. "And this is my traveling companion, Joses."

"Come in, please. We are in the midst of praying, actually." She led them down a corridor into a great room where two handfuls of people rose to greet them.

"These are followers of Jesus in Rome. There are others scattered throughout the city, but we have to be cautious in our

gatherings. That is why I asked you about the second miracle."
She nodded to a man standing to her left. "And this is my husband, Aquila. We lead this church."

So many words to say, so much to recount, but in this moment, Phoebe contented herself by sitting on a bench, giving her feet a rest, while Priscilla made all the introductions.

"There will be plenty of time to talk," Aquila said. "But now you look travel weary. Sit, rest, eat, and then we will gladly hear your story." He offered them wine and stew, what she called an *agape* feast. Breaking bread with these strangers, Phoebe reveled in the strange fact that Jesus was not merely Lord in Cenchreae, but in all the world, because each person in the room hailed from somewhere other than Rome. When they lifted their voices in song, different languages wafted to the ceiling, a pleasing aroma to the Almighty, she knew.

One person brought a word from the Lord—about persevering during persecution. Another shared how God had met a very specific financial need. Another asked that they all pray for her son who was imprisoned.

"And now, let us hear from our guests," Priscilla said.

Phoebe realized she had not yet taken off her satchel, so she did so now, letting the weight of it finally, truly, be released from her shoulders. "I am Phoebe," she said. "And I have been on a long journey to bring you a gift from the apostle Paul in Cenchreae."

Priscilla let out a gasp. "Our apostle Paul? You know him?"

She nodded. "He entrusted me with this lengthy letter—written with passion and love for all of you."

Priscilla, seemingly unashamed, cried. "At last," she finally said.

"Amen," said Aquila. He turned to Joses. "And you were part of this journey, I assume?"

"Yes," Joses said. "Paul asked me to accompany Phoebe, to protect her along the journey. We were three in the beginning, but her servant Trecia left us partway through. We would covet your prayers for her welfare."

"Though we are eager to hear the words of our dear, dear friend," Priscilla said, "I feel compelled to pray for your companion. Trecia, is it?"

"Thank you," Phoebe said. "I am very worried about her."

The group of believers knelt on the cobbles of the large room, their prayers rising to the heavenly realms, where Jesus considered it His privilege to intercede for the saints day in and day out. Oh the glory of prayer with those who loved Him so! Phoebe could barely contain her joy. What began with collapsed tears upon the entrance into this place progressed to deep-seated joy.

Finally, Phoebe spoke. "I have been with Paul when he spoke these words, as a scribe recorded them. He has taken great pains to detail the importance of the Gospel, and he has shown me the gift of his inflection." She opened the scroll, its seal finally broken, and cleared her throat. She thought back to the time Paul said these words initially, his eyes dancing, and his hands gesturing with great joy. Whenever he spoke of the Gospel, he could not contain himself. She pictured him then and prepared her heart to emulate the reading just as he would.

"'Paul, a servant of Christ Jesus, called to be an apostle and set apart for the gospel of God—the gospel he promised beforehand through his prophets in the Holy Scriptures regarding his Son, who as to his earthly life was a descendant of David, and who through the Spirit of holiness was appointed the Son of God in power by his resurrection from the dead: Jesus Christ our Lord. Through him we received grace and apostleship to call all the Gentiles to the obedience that comes from faith for his name's sake. And you also are among those Gentiles who are called to belong to Jesus Christ,'" she read.

Priscilla and Aquila held hands, eyes moist.

Phoebe continued, "'First, I thank my God through Jesus Christ for all of you, because your faith is being reported all over the world. God, whom I serve in my spirit in preaching the gospel of his Son, is my witness how constantly I remember you in my prayers at all times; and I pray that now at last by God's will the way may be opened for me to come to you. I long to see you so that I may impart to you some spiritual gift to make you strong—that is, that you and I may be mutually encouraged by each other's faith. I do not want you to be unaware, brothers and sisters, that I planned many times to come to you (but have been prevented from doing so until now) in order that I might have a harvest among you, just as I have had among the other Gentiles. I am obligated both to Greeks and non-Greeks, both to the wise and the foolish. That is why I am so eager to preach the gospel also to you who are in Rome.'"

"He is coming to see us?" Priscilla asked.

"That is his intention," Phoebe responded. "The Holy Spirit has been whispering Spain into his heart and mind. If the Lord wills, he will stop by here on his way there."

"I pray he is not disappointed in us when he comes. We had hoped to have more people by now, but the work is arduous," Aquila said. "This Roman soil, it is hard ground. We are breaking up the fallow to find the fruit. So much hard-heartedness. So much self-sufficiency. While there are many idols and little gods aplenty here, I would say the greatest barrier to the Gospel is ease. No one seems to need help from the heavens."

"It is the same around the empire," Joses said. "Particularly when money is involved. Those who have no lack have no need for the eternal. It is those whose desperation is elevated who grab at anything to fill them. Unfortunately, they do not always find solace in the great Gospel of Jesus."

"Well, it is comfort, though in an unexpected way, that others are experiencing the same kinds of barriers and temptations as we are. We are not alone, as evidenced by the two of you in our midst. I can only imagine your journey to bring these words to us."

Priscilla smiled and placed her hand upon Aquila's knee. "We want to hear that story, but we are starved for the words of Paul. Please, Phoebe, continue your discourse. We want to hear everything. No matter how late the hour, we thirst for words like these. You are slaking our need."

So Phoebe continued reading about sin, the heartache of God, the waywardness of humankind, the great love of Jesus in the midst of it all, the inability of the Law to save everyone, the resurrection of Christ, how one must respond to the government, and all the nuances of God's grace as it influenced the Body. They began the evening with a love feast, and they ended it with a word feast, relishing every intonation, every jot, every tittle. Her eyes misted when she read the words Paul had spoken like a prayer over her when the journey began, "'I commend to you our sister Phoebe, who is a deacon in the church in Cenchreae. Welcome her in the Lord as one who is worthy of honor among God's people. Help her in whatever she needs, for she has been helpful to many, and especially to me.'"

"Thank you for embarking on such a perilous journey for our sakes," Priscilla added.

"It has been my supreme pleasure, the greatest adventure of my life." She caught the gaze of Joses, wondering what his future meant, how he would make his way in the world in light of his revelations. She had grown fond of the man. "And now," she said, "there are words for this body from the hand of Paul. He writes, 'Greet Priscilla and Aquila, my co-workers in Christ Jesus. They risked their lives for me. Not only I but all the churches of the Gentiles are grateful to them. Greet also the church that meets at their house.'"

A cheer erupted from the small group. "That is us," a haggard-looking man said, his voice quavering with age but his smile as youthful as new spring growth.

"I am grateful beyond words," Aquila said, "that Paul considers us colaborers in the Gospel. That has always been how I saw things, and he never, ever lorded his prestige over us, but simply came alongside, training us to plant churches. He has been my dearest friend." He wiped tears from his eyes. "Now if only he would come and visit as he longs to. That would complete my joy."

Joses asked, "How did you risk your lives for Paul?"

"We were with him in Ephesus when amazing things began to happen," Aquila said. "Seven sons of Sceva used the name of Jesus to cast out demons. But they did not know Him or honor Him as Lord. So when they used Jesus in their power encounters with darkness, it was reported that a demon responded with something like 'I know Jesus, and I know Paul, but who are you?' The man who had been oppressed suddenly jumped on the men, then overpowered them. They ran from the house naked and bruised. This caused the name of Jesus to be feared and honored, and it opened the doorway for more ministry."

"The audacity of those men," Priscilla said. "To think Jesus's name could be used as incantation without relationship. To us it felt like the epitome of taking God's name in vain." She shook her head. "But the whole encounter seemed to open up a pathway for us to share more freely. This worked well until Demetrius roused himself in anger."

"I believe I have heard Paul use his name but not in an affable way," Phoebe said.

"I am sure that must be true." Priscilla looked at the other believers gathered in her home. "I do not believe I have shared this story yet. Would you like to hear it?"

A girl, probably fourteen, nodded vigorously. "Yes, please do," she said, face upturned.

"Demetrius was a silversmith who made his wealth out of fashioning shrines and mementos of the Greek goddess Artemis. He employed many, so he gathered them all together in hopes of inciting a riot."

"Why?" Joses asked.

"People meeting Jesus meant an abandonment of goddess worship, and, therefore, an end to a lucrative business," Aquila said.

"So he rallied his workers with something to the effect of 'Our wealth depends on making handiwork for the sake of Artemis, but this Paul fellow has blasphemed our gods, saying Artemis is not really a goddess after all. He's stirred the entire world with words like this.' Although his primary motivation was economic, he was a clever man who understood the audience he spoke to, so he stirred them up by saying Paul would destroy the influence of Artemis, and that she would lose world renown and respect."

"That is all he needed to say," Aquila said. "The crowd that erupted began chanting, 'Great is Artemis of the Ephesians!' The crowd swelled and rushed to the amphitheater, dragging our fellow companions Gaius and Aristarchus with them. We were almost toppled in the melee, and I had to hold tightly to Priscilla's hand so she would not be trampled to death. Paul tried to follow, but we strongly urged him to stay back from the crowd, fearing his demise. Everyone yelled, cursed, and wagged their heads, and we believed this would certainly be the end of our lives. But Paul? He remained calm. Finally the mayor quieted the crowd. He said they were being rash and frenzied. Of course Artemis and her reputation could not be thwarted. He told them to calm down."

Priscilla motioned with her arms, raising them, then lowering them, showing how the mayor got the attention of the mob. "He reminded the crowd that we had stolen nothing, and that the matter could be settled as a legal matter, not in a mob. Paul seemed unfazed by any of it. He simply went about the remaining work of encouraging the new local believers, then left unceremoniously for Macedonia."

"That is just how Paul did things," Aquila said. "His trust in the Spirit's prompting and provision trumped all fear. We were utterly privileged to walk alongside him, make tents as we paid for our ministry, and pray with him. Oh, how I miss him."

"I do too," Phoebe said.

They spent the rest of the evening reminiscing, telling stories, and getting acquainted. They prayed together, then Priscilla led Phoebe to a small chamber where a well-made bed waited in the corner. She nearly cried at the sight of it. "I do not know how to thank you—for the meal, your kindness, all of it. But this bed? It looks like heaven to me."

Priscilla laughed. "You flatter me. It is my joy to serve you. It is as if I am serving my friend Paul, and, in turn, I am serving Jesus. Thank you for the privilege. Now, rest up. We have much to do tomorrow. We must find scribes to make copies for the other churches."

At this, Phoebe's heart fell. She had no more wealth to finance such an endeavor. "I am afraid I have bad news," she told Priscilla.

"What do you mean?"

"I have no more resources with me. They all reside in Cenchreae. The voyage, the robbery, the journey by foot—all these together took everything I had taken with me."

Priscilla laughed again. "Denarii are nothing to our Almighty God. Do not dread the morning, dear Phoebe. Anticipate it. Instead, we will see how God will supply all our needs according to His riches. He is a wealthy God who created everything we see. He owns every animal, every tree, every strain of gold. We will take to our knees again in the morning, seeking His provision. But presently? You must sleep."

When Priscilla left, taking her candle with her, the room suddenly shifted into the blackest night. The coverlet upon Phoebe's bed smelled of sunshine, and soon she drifted into blessed, comfortable sleep.

CHAPTER TWENTY-EIGHT

Sunlight angled into her room, landing on Phoebe's field of vision. Hues of orange and pink beckoned her to the day. She breathed in the scent of wisteria, or was it roses? For that time between sleep and wakefulness, she fancied herself home. She sat on the edge of the bed and dressed herself—without Trecia. That familiar ache rose up in her. Where was her friend, her companion? Was she safe? She prayed again for Trecia—an impossible sort of prayer to the God who rescues.

In the courtyard, many people buzzed about. These were not the faces of last night but a different crowd altogether—laborers who made tents under the supervision of Aquila. Instead of a circle of fellowship, theirs was a bustling of tables, canvas, and tools she was not acquainted with. Aquila briefly told her about their enterprise when Priscilla interrupted them. "Phoebe needs to eat," she said.

And eat, she did. All that deprivation had shrunk her stomach, but this morning, she found her appetite roaring back to life, and she feasted on curds, honey, dried meat, and grapes. When satisfied, she thanked Priscilla. "I need to talk to Joses," she said.

But Priscilla said nothing, and her face registered something Phoebe could not discern. "What is it?"

She handed Phoebe a small scroll. "Aquila found this upon his bed this morning. I am afraid he has left."

Oh, please help, God! Without taking the scroll, she ran throughout the house, completely forgetting propriety, yelling his name. "Joses, where are you?" But her voice simply echoed off walls, and no one answered back.

Priscilla caught up with her. "I am so sorry." She pulled Phoebe into an embrace, while Phoebe tried not to cry, but it was no use. Tears answered, while her time with Joses flashed before her—his persistence, kindness, and faithfulness. She had kept him at a calculated distance, and now when he created his own distance, she suddenly realized what was lost. All her grief mingled through her—losing her parents, dear Albus, her home, and poor Trecia. And now another. She struggled to talk while Priscilla soothed her.

"Ours is a ministry of goodbyes," she told Phoebe. "And I know all too well the pain of it all. But perhaps he has written words that will soothe you. Will you not sit?" She directed Phoebe to a long couch along a sunny courtyard. "I will leave you to read it alone." Phoebe thanked her new companion whose footfalls echoed down the corridor.

Phoebe looked at the scroll, rolled it through her hands, wondering what words would come from it. She feared the revelations. Nevertheless, she unfurled it, took a deep breath, and read.

> *Phoebe of Cenchreae,*
> *I must ask for your forgiveness for leaving in haste before the dawn, but my conscience would not allow me to stay any*

longer. I know it would go poorly for me if my master's servants throughout the empire find me first. Instead, I must return to him to face whatever painful consequences he will dole out. I will endeavor to locate Paul in the middle of the journey, to tell him everything that has transpired. It will be a time of confession on my part. Once I shared my burden with you yesterday, the light cleansed me from the inside out. For so long, I believed if I told my secrets, only darkness and shame would prevail. I did not realize how the lies inside controlled my temperament. You have given me a shred of freedom simply by listening.

I have made arrangements with Aquila for another to accompany you back to Cenchreae to honor my commitment to return you safely. He will give you further details.

On my journey to Macedonia, I will also make inquiries of your Trecia. Perhaps God will look upon my search with blessing, and I shall find her. Please pray for a favorable outcome.

If I see Paul, the first thing I will do is confess my sin. And then I will ask for his forgiveness because I betrayed both you and him. I will be sure to recount your bravery, the plight of Trecia, and your successfully completed mission. I will reflect back to him how the believers here in Rome were moved by his words, and how Priscilla and Aquila practically shone in the light of their mutual friendship. I hope to share well, giving the story the justice it deserves.

I am proud of you, as a brother is proud of his sister's accomplishments. You have endured much. You have lost much. You have loved much. And I am all the richer for having met

you and companioned alongside you. I do hope our pathways
cross again in this life, but if not, we will see each other in the
sweet hereafter—God willing.

  Joses

So much to take in. But it was Joses's honesty that shone
through, and his repentant heart. Oh that he would be safe, and
that his master would err on the side of mercy rather than justice.

She rerolled the scroll, letting the words permeate her
heart. The entire journey replayed itself in her mind. Phoebe
wiped away a tear, then another. Then she knelt on the stone
floor, her torso bent over the low-lying couch, and prayed for
Joses with everything she had. She prayed he would meet Paul
before he met his master, and see her again on the other side
of heaven's glory. "Thank You, God," she prayed, "for the odd
ways You work. If I were to fashion this journey, I would not
have saddled me with a servant girl who deserted us or given
me a runaway slave as protection. I certainly would not have
had sea raiders insert themselves into the voyage. But You, my
Lord, are sovereign, and Your plans are far better and different
than I can imagine. And, in the end, the scroll has made it to
its home, I am alive, and I have made new friends. I have
learned of Your beautiful companionship to me—a widow.
And as a wealthy woman, I was forced to learn dependence on
You. All of this is sheer gift. You are my gift. And I love You
even more today than when I left Cenchreae on this journey."

Priscilla touched her shoulder, saying a quiet amen. She
pulled Phoebe to her feet. "We have much work to do," she said.

Footsteps clattered on the stone floor, and a flurry of commotion like the sound of geese fluttered down the corridor. Priscilla gave Phoebe a puzzled look. "I wonder what that is about."

They rushed toward the noise coming from the atrium.

There stood a disheveled Trecia.

Beautiful Trecia.

Phoebe ran to her and pulled her into a heaving embrace. She touched her hair, held her tight, while Trecia's cries muffled into Phoebe's shoulder. Eternity lived in that moment, and it took Phoebe a long time to pull away and look at her companion's face. "You are here," she finally said.

"I am so sorry." Trecia wept. "I should have listened to your warnings about Longinus."

Priscilla directed them toward a quiet alcove covered in vines and brought cups of cool water as they sat on stone benches opposite each other.

"Are you all right?" Phoebe asked.

"I am now." Trecia pulled in a long breath. "How can you ever forgive me?"

"It is already done. I was more broken than angry, and my heart was full of worry for your safety. But here you are— sitting before me. It is a miracle."

Trecia nodded. Her hair, unkempt, sheltered a sunburned forehead. She fiddled with her hands on her lap, covered in bruises and blood.

"What happened, dear Trecia?"

Trecia spilled her story, in short snippets at first, cascading into a powerful narrative of God's deliverance. Longinus originally told her they would use their map to find Priscilla and Aquila in hopes of robbing them, and then, with their newly acquired "wealth," they would finally live together in matrimony. They had traveled north, along the same road Joses and Phoebe walked, but with a lead. "I tried to dissuade him from robbery. You have to believe me," she said.

"I do." Phoebe reached out and held Trecia's bruised hands in hers.

"And I memorized the map whenever he pulled it out, Phoebe. I sensed the Spirit tell me to do it."

"I am glad you did."

"Outside of Rome, Longinus turned his affection into wickedness. He kept up the ruse long enough to keep me walking northward." She lowered her voice when she spoke of his laugh as he sold her to a brothel and pocketed the money with glee. The purchasers knew him well and asked him for more girls as soon as possible.

"I had only been a means to acquire money," Trecia said. Later, chained to a basement room's wall, Trecia cried out for deliverance. None came for several days. She spoke of other girls being called upstairs, and their echoing cries of terror as they ascended the stone steps. When the girl chained next to her was taken, Trecia realized her shackles were not as tight as she thought. She pressed her thumbs toward her little fingers, making her hands as tiny as she could, and eventually wrested herself free. "I had no sense of day or night, but when I snuck upstairs and crept out of the building, a starry sky greeted me."

"What did you do next?"

"I wound my way through Rome's streets, praying and straining to remember the map Longinus stole. Dawn came, and terror strangled me. I worried that the men who shackled me would surely find me. But then I found this place, and here I am."

"Thank God."

Trecia looked long into Phoebe's eyes then pulled in a breath. "Where is Joses?"

"The Spirit compelled him back home. But do not worry. We will stay here as you recover and I find scribes to make copies of Paul's letter. Then another man will accompany us home—that is, if you want to return with me."

"That is the only journey I want to take," Trecia said.

They walked hand in hand down the corridors of Priscilla and Aquila's tent-making enterprise as roses scented their way. The sun, high in the sky's midpoint, cast light like a hymn of praise.

Phoebe felt the accomplishment of a completed task rise up within her, and as the next journey stretched before her and Trecia, she wanted nothing more than to see again the shining eyes of the apostle who entrusted her with such a sacred task.

Lord willing.

FACTS BEHIND
the Fiction

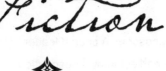

BACHELOR PAUL, THE CHURCH STARTER

"He was a man of middling size, and his hair was scanty, and his legs were a little crooked, and his knees were projecting, and he had large eyes and his eyebrows met, and his nose was somewhat long, and he was full of grace and mercy."

—A description of Paul from
Acts of Paul and Thecla, AD 100s

FACIAL COMPOSITE OF SAINT PAUL CREATED
BY EXPERTS USING HISTORICAL SOURCES

Paul wasn't handsome. A church leader said so in the earliest known description of Paul, written in an apocryphal book called *Acts of Paul and Thecla*. The apostle John fired the author, who confessed to writing that book. This firing was recounted in an ancient news report from Tertullian (AD 155–240), a Christian writer in North Africa.

If Tertullian got history right, Apostle John may not have been as concerned about the unflattering portrait of Paul as he was about the book's claim that Paul taught abstinence.

Paul was a celibate bachelor and proud of it. "I wish that all of you were like me.... But if you don't have enough self-control, then go ahead and get married" (1 Corinthians 7:7, 9 CEV).

WHAT WE KNOW
ABOUT PAUL

· Born in the city of Tarsus in what is now Turkey in about AD 5

· Lifelong Roman citizen because Rome had declared Tarsus a free city in 42 BC

· Educated by Gamaliel, a leading Pharisee in Jerusalem

· Converted to Christianity after seeing a vision of Jesus

· Helped introduce the Jewish movement of Christianity to non-Jews

· Started church groups in Syria, Cyprus, Turkey, Greece, and possibly Spain

· Worked as a tent maker, as needed, to help support himself and his ministry

· Traditionally credited with writing almost half the books in the New Testament—thirteen of the twenty-seven. (Although some scholars credit him with writing just eight.)

· Reportedly beheaded in Rome during the mid-60s AD.

PAUL'S ENEMIES

One particular group of people caused Paul the most consternation: "Judaizers" (JEW-day-eye-zurs) is what people of the time called them. They got that name because they were Jewish converts to Christianity who tried to Judaize the Christian religion. It makes sense that they would want to do so because Christianity started as a Jewish movement, and Jesus and all His disciples were Jews.

Judaizers thought of Christianity as another branch of the Jewish religion—an alternative "denomination" for Jews. Sadducees emphasized the written laws of Moses. Pharisees emphasized extra nonwritten laws passed down from rabbis by oral tradition from one generation to the next. Christians emphasized Jesus as the Messiah.

Paul taught that non-Jewish Christians didn't have to obey the uniquely Jewish laws. This included laws of Moses, which required all Jews to observe the kosher food restrictions and that all Jewish men must be circumcised.

Judaizers disagreed with Paul, even after a Jerusalem council meeting of leaders sided with Paul (Acts 15). Some Judaizers went so far as to follow Paul on his missionary trips. After Paul left town, they would go into any church group Paul had created. There, they said that anyone who wanted to be a Christian follower of the Jewish Messiah needed to observe the same Jewish laws Paul did.

This upset Paul, because these Jewish Christians were convincing non-Jews that Christianity had joined the Jewish faith. Paul taught the opposite: that Jews had joined the Christian faith.

"The Law was our teacher," Paul explained. "It was supposed to teach us until we had faith and were acceptable to God.... Faith in Christ Jesus is what makes each of you equal with each other, whether you are a Jew or a Greek, a slave or a free person, a man or a woman" (Galatians 3:24, 28 CEV).

Animosity between the two groups of Christians eventually grew so toxic that Jewish leaders decided to ban Jewish Christians from the synagogue. That forced those Jews to make a choice between the two religions. Most Jews, it seems, returned to their traditional roots and to the synagogue. Christianity soon became a predominantly non-Jewish religion.

Today, Jews make up about 1 percent of Christians in the world. Out of about fifteen million Jews in the world, less than two million call themselves Christian (Pew Research Center, 2013). There are more than two billion people who call themselves Christians.

PAUL PROBABLY SAILED ON A SHIP VERY MUCH LIKE THIS ONE

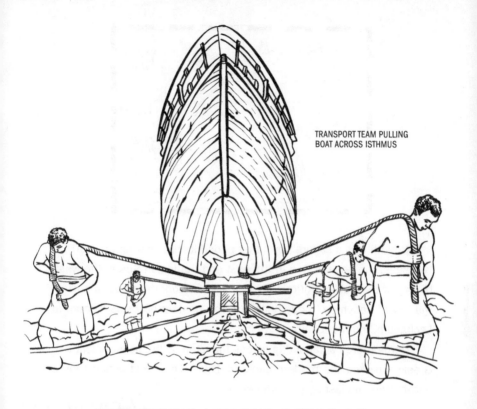

TRANSPORT TEAM PULLING
BOAT ACROSS ISTHMUS

PHOEBE'S NEIGHBORHOOD:
BOATS ON WHEELS

Sailors of Phoebe's time and home took an odd shortcut around the southern tip of Greece. Instead of risking sudden, gale-force winds or pirates by sailing some 350 miles (560 km) around the Peloponnese peninsula, they hitched a ride on a flatbed wagon called the Crossing Machine, *Diolkos* in Greek.

Transport teams hauled merchant ships and warships on a stone-paved road across the four-mile-wide (6 km) isthmus, a little north of the city of Corinth. Sometimes they'd haul just the cargo, and then load it onto another ship waiting on the other side. Emperor Augustus used this method during a civil war to expedite his pursuit of Marc Antony, who fled to Cleopatra in Egypt.

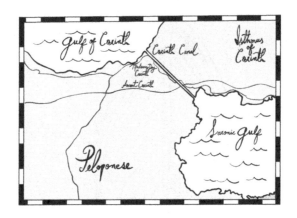

Corinth was a sailors' town that prided itself in having two ports in two seas: the Aegean Sea in the east and the Ionian Sea in the west, by way of the Gulf of Corinth. Phoebe lived in Corinth's eastern port, in the city of Cenchrae, today Kechries. The western port was located at Lechaeum, today Lechaio.

Nero ordered a canal dug across the isthmus but never finished it. Greeks finished the modern canal in 1893. The construction took a dozen years of blasting through bedrock.

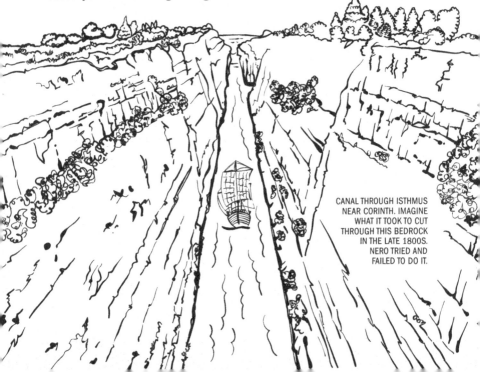

CANAL THROUGH ISTHMUS NEAR CORINTH. IMAGINE WHAT IT TOOK TO CUT THROUGH THIS BEDROCK IN THE LATE 1800S. NERO TRIED AND FAILED TO DO IT.

NEIGHBORHOOD HOUSE CHURCHES

Jews worshipped in the Jerusalem temple and in synagogues scattered in cities throughout the Roman Empire. But for Christians, there was no sacred space anywhere uniquely devoted to worship.

Christians couldn't build a church, because Rome declared Christianity illegal. Romans had many misconceptions about Christians. For one, when Romans heard about the ritual of communion, or the Eucharist, and about people partaking of the body and blood of Christ, they presumed Christians were cannibals.

Christians were arrested and executed in Nero's terrible first wave of persecution, in the mid-60s. This sent the early Christians into hiding, and they began to worship secretly in homes.

RECONSTRUCTION OF PETER'S HOUSE
IN CAPERNAUM, WHICH MAY HAVE
SERVED AS A HOUSE CHURCH

Initially, it seems, local church leaders were the people who hosted the meetings in their homes. The apostle Paul mentions several. He sent greetings to "Aquila and Priscilla, together with the church that meets in their house" (1 Corinthians 16:19 CEV). Likewise a woman in what is now Turkey: "Nympha and the church that meets in her home" (Colossians 4:15 CEV). And again to "Philemon...and to the church that meets in your home" (Philemon 1:1–2 CEV).

Inevitably, some hosts began to move away from the apostles' teaching. John called out one:

"Diotrephes likes to be the number-one leader, and he won't pay any attention to us....He has been attacking us with gossip.... He refuses to welcome any of the Lord's followers who come by. And when other church members want to welcome them, he puts them out of the church" (3 John 1:9–10 CEV).

The apostles considered themselves chief administrators of local church leaders, who were known by various names: overseers, bishops, elders, presbyters, deacons, and deaconesses.

Paul wrote his friend Timothy, in the coastal city of Ephesus in what is now Turkey, and gave him a list of characteristics to look for when selecting local church leaders.

Overseer/bishop. "They must be self-controlled, sensible, well-behaved, friendly to strangers, and able to teach....[T]hey must be kind and gentle and not love money" (1 Timothy 3:2–3 CEV).

Deacons (Paul used the Greek word *diakonos* to describe men and women). "They must first prove themselves. Then if no one has anything against them, they can serve as officers" (1 Timothy 3:10 CEV).

Some local leaders set forth their own ideas and started their own sects. One leader, Tatian, created his own Gospel of Jesus by harmonizing the four Gospels of Matthew, Mark, Luke, and John into one book.

This alarmed many church leaders. By the AD 90s, local church leaders started clamoring for top leaders to be appointed based on their faith and on credentials linking them to the apostles.

This led to the emergence of bishops, including the Bishop of Rome, better known as the Pope.

PETER'S HOUSE CHURCH

Archaeologists say they are confident that they found the first-century house church that belonged to Peter. He lived in Capernaum, the fishing village Jesus used as the headquarters for his ministry.

Archaeologists say that soon after the resurrection and ascension of Jesus, Peter's simple house with its rough walls got a makeover. Someone plastered the main meeting room from floor to ceiling. They also inscribed Christian sayings onto the walls: "Lord Jesus, help your servant" and "Christ, have mercy." Archaeologists say this makeover suggests that people in the community met here for worship.

After Rome legalized Christianity in the AD 300s, Christians started building churches, including an octagonal church built over the ruins of Peter's home. Visitors to the ruins of Capernaum today can see the eight-sided ruins of that church, which was located just a few steps away from the city synagogue, where it's believed Jesus once taught and healed people.

Fiction Author
MARY DEMUTH

Mary DeMuth is an international speaker and podcaster, and she's the novelist and nonfiction author of thirty-nine books, including *We Too: How the Church Can Respond Redemptively to the Sexual Abuse Crisis.* She loves to help people re-story their lives. She lives in Texas with her husband of twenty-nine years and is the mom to three adult children. Find out more at marydemuth. com, or be prayed for on her daily prayer podcast pray-everyday.show. For sexual abuse resources, visit wetoo.org.

Nonfiction Author
STEPHEN M. MILLER

Stephen M. Miller is an award-winning, best-selling Christian author of easy-reading books about the Bible and Christianity. His books have sold over 1.9 million copies and include *The Complete Guide to the Bible, Who's Who and Where's Where in the Bible,* and *How to Get Into the Bible.*

Miller lives in the suburbs of Kansas City with his wife, Linda, a registered nurse. They have two married children who live nearby.

Read on for a sneak peek of another exciting story
in the Ordinary Women of the Bible series!

PURSUED BY A KING: ABIGAIL'S STORY

by Elizabeth Adams and Diana Wallis Taylor

Abigail enjoyed the feeling of the sun on her skin as she walked to the marketplace. After so many weeks indoors, it felt wonderful to feel its warmth again.

Anna quickened her steps to keep up. "Mistress, you must slow down. You need to be careful of your health."

"I feel fine." Abigail stepped to the side to let a woman trailed by small children pass. "The fever has passed."

"But you do not yet have your strength back."

Abigail knew she should be grateful for Anna's fretting. She was loyal and kind, and Abigail didn't know what she would do without her. Abigail also knew Anna had been right to be worried, as she had just fought off the same fever that had taken her mother several years ago. But sometimes her maid needed to simply trust that Abigail knew her own condition.

"I am hoping to find a nice fish for *Abba*'s supper. You are so good at selecting the best choices, so I will value your help in choosing."

The words seemed to placate Anna, who straightened up a bit as she fell into step behind her mistress. Abigail needed tonight's dinner to go well. She had thought of her plan as she lay on her mat so many nights, fighting the fever, and tonight she hoped to make it happen.

"Let's look at the vegetables," Anna said, gesturing at the stalls piled high with squash and cucumbers and melons. She selected some squash, since they had already eaten all their garden had supplied. Abigail and Anna threaded through the narrow alleys, past merchants calling out about the wonders of their fruits and cooking pots and rugs. It was hot, dusty, and loud, with too many colors, sights, and sounds all fighting for her attention. Abigail loved it. She looked around for the rug merchant's son, but she did not see him at his family's stall. She had first noticed Ira many months back, during the rainy season, and Abigail had approached the stall, pretending she was in need of a rug, to get a closer look. He appeared to be a few years older than she, and very handsome. And he had been kind, and his voice deep and rich, as he showed her the many fine rugs on offer. She suspected he had known she wasn't really looking for a rug, and when she had turned to go, he had urged her to come back and see the new rugs they would have the next week. She had come again the next week, and the week after that, and even when she could not stop to see his wares, she had met his eye across the marketplace many times. It always sent a surge of excitement through her. But he was not there today. She had not been to market in several weeks. Had something happened to him in that time?

At the spice dealers, she purchased some capers to go with mint from their garden, as well as costly saffron. From the grain merchant, she bought millet and walnuts. For dessert, she bought more honey and pomegranates for one of her father's favorite desserts, pomegranate and poached apricots in honey syrup.

"Mistress, do you know that man?"

"Who?" Abigail had just placed the fruit in a bag and handed it to Anna, and then she looked up to see who Anna was talking about.

"That man over there." Anna was looking across the crowded market to a group of men standing in the shade of the covered portico. A woman led a mule piled with wares past, blocking the men for a moment.

"I do not see who you mean."

"The tall one in the middle there. He keeps looking at you." The woman and the mule passed, and the men came into view again. "I saw him when we were looking at the spices, and here he is again. He is watching you."

Abigail saw who she meant now. He was looking right at her. He was handsome, in a rough way, with his dark beard and hair that curled to his shoulders. He was well dressed—a man of means—and she guessed him to be many years her elder. She had not seen him before. Still looking at her, the man spoke to the merchant in the stall next to him and then nodded his head. Then he inclined his head towards her, a hint of a smile curving his lips.

Abigail turned and started to thread her way through the crowded alleyway once again. "I do not know him." Something about the way he was looking at her made her uneasy. They made their way past the merchants selling richly dyed fabrics and heaping piles of grains, but she could still feel his eyes on her. She glanced back, and saw that he was still looking her way. "Let us go, Anna. I feel I am more tired than I thought."

Anna shook her head, but did not say that she'd warned her. Abigail led them through the crowded marketplace, back past the rug merchant's stall once again. Ira was still not there, and she felt a pang of disappointment.

No matter. It would not change her plans for this evening. As they passed a fruit merchant's stall, Abigail saw the small hand of a child dart out and grab a few figs. It did not register as strange until the booming voice of the merchant rang out.

"Stop!"

Abigail saw the young boy, the fruit still clutched in his hand, trying to run past her, but the man from the next stall, the man who sold olive oil in earthenware jugs, grabbed the boy by his cloak and held him.

"Give back the figs," the fruit seller said. His face was twisted up in anger.

Abigail saw it then. The boy was trembling, and so thin his clothes hung off him. He was hungry. And though she knew she should not do it, though she heard her father's voice begging her to keep her tongue and think before she acted, she could not stop the words that came out.

"Thank you, Ira." It was the first name that came to mind, and she flushed, hoping no one would understand why. But she went on. "You got the figs I requested. Let me see them."

The boy looked up at her with wide eyes. She nodded at him, silently urging him to play along, and slowly he uncurled his fingers. The fruit seller shifted his feet, watching, but his face still wore a scowl. Anna stood a few paces away, and Abigail recognized the look in her eye. She was silently begging Abigail to walk away before she got herself in trouble. Loyal Anna. Abigail turned back to the boy.

"You have chosen well. Those will go nicely with Abba's meal." She looked up at the fruit seller, a wide smile on her face. "How much do I owe?"

The fruit seller looked from her to the boy and back again. He did not believe her, that much was clear. But he dared not contradict her either. Slowly, seemingly unsure of what to do, he named a price. It was ludicrously high, at least three times what the figs were worth, but Abigail did not flinch. She reached into her dress, pulled out her small bag of coins, and handed them over. The fruit seller continued to watch her warily, but the other man let go of the boy's clothing.

"Next time, you must tell the man I am coming with payment before you leave the stall," she said to the boy, extending the farce. He nodded, his eyes still wide. "Come," she said, her voice cheerful. "Let us continue on."

The boy followed, still clutching the figs, until they were out of sight of the fruit merchant. Then Abigail stopped and turned to the boy.

"You are hungry."

He nodded.

"How many of you are there?"

"I have three younger sisters." His voice came out quietly, faltering.

"Where is your mother?"

"The fever took her."

The words hit Abigail hard. She bit her lip, looking up at the clear blue sky. Then, when she had calmed herself enough to speak, she said, "I am sorry to hear it." She gestured for Anna to hand her the bag, and reluctantly, her servant did. Abigail reached in and pulled out the fruit she had purchased for her father's supper, as well as the fish, wrapped in cloth, and the honey and walnuts.

"Take these," she said. "For your sisters."

The boy did not argue. He was probably too hungry to think of it. "Thank you."

"You know how to cook it?"

He nodded.

"Good." Abigail gazed around. She did not see the fruit merchant anywhere, but she did not believe the boy was safe here. "Now, it is probably best for you to leave this place before those men find you."

He ducked his head and turned, and in a few moments had vanished into the crowd. Abigail turned back to Anna.

"It appears we will need to do our shopping all over again."

Anna did not say anything for a moment. Her lips were pursed. Abigail knew she did not approve of what had just happened. Anna was good and true, a rule follower. She was much like Abigail's father in that way. Beyond that, she worried about Abigail. Anna loved her like her own child, and she had served

Abigail her whole life. She did not approve of anything that put Abigail in harm's way. But now, Anna simply followed Abigail, walking behind her as she returned to the same stalls she had visited shortly before.

It was not until they were back on the road and walking toward home that Anna spoke. "That was foolish, mistress. Anything could have happened to you."

"He was hungry. It would have been cruel not to help him."

"He was getting the punishment he deserved. It is not your place to feed all the thieves and liars in the market."

"He is a *child*, Anna. A child with no mother, and many sisters to feed."

"Still. It is not your place. You must learn to think before you act."

Abigail knew she would get nowhere with her maid, so she let the conversation drop. But she continued the discussion inside her own mind. If it wasn't her place to help, whose place was it? Hadn't Yahweh commanded them not to glean the edges of the fields but leave some for the poor? What was that if not a command to care about those too poor to feed themselves?

As they walked, their feet stirring up fine red dust, she shifted her thinking to what she would say to her father over dinner tonight. She had mentioned Ira to her father several times, speaking of his kindness and the way he made her laugh, so he knew who Ira was. The rug-maker's family was in good standing in the village. She was of marriageable age, she would remind him. Many of the girls she had known as a child were already married, and some even had babies of their own.

It was time for her father to arrange a betrothal for her, she would insist. And Ira was kind, and from a good family. His father did well in business. He was also funny, and the way he smiled at her made her stomach feel warm. Tonight she would feed her father well, and after he had had some wine and was feeling relaxed, she would suggest that Ira would make a good husband.

Their steward, Remiel, met them at the door when they arrived home, and he took the items they had purchased from Abigail.

"It is well you have returned, mistress," Remiel said. There was an expression on his face that she couldn't read. "We have a guest, and your father has been anxious to speak with you."

Abigail handed her mantle to Anna and straightened her veil. Was it Ira? Was that why he had not been in the market? She pinched her cheeks to give them color and then walked to the main room that overlooked the courtyard. When she saw him, she stopped suddenly and took a quick breath. The man standing next to her father was the man from the marketplace. The one who had been watching her.

"Daughter, we have been anxious for your return. You must meet our guest."

Abba put his arm around her shoulders. "Abigail, this is Nabal. He is from Maon."

Nabal nodded to her. "If you will forgive me, I was quite taken with you in the marketplace, and learned you were the daughter of someone I have done business with for many years. He is a most fortunate man to have such a beautiful daughter."

Abigail felt uneasy with his praise. Why was he here? She smiled briefly, acknowledging his words, but remained silent, looking to her father and then the stranger. Abigail's father was in the business of wool. What did this man have to do with that?

"It is nice to meet you," she said. And then she quickly continued, "Please excuse me. I must speak with the cook and then prepare myself for our evening meal. Will you be joining us?"

"Most assuredly. Your father has kindly invited me to remain for the night. I must return to my estate in Maon in the morning."

An estate? He was indeed a man of means, then. She bowed her head and walked to the room at the back of the house to speak to the cook. She tried to hide her disappointment. She could not speak to her father about Ira if this man was here. Tonight's special meal would be a waste.

Several hours later, they sat on the mats and enjoyed the richly prepared meal—squash with capers and mint, saffroned millet with raisins and walnuts, and fresh bread with goat cheese. Nabal praised the meal, and spoke to Abigail's father of his fertile land and his success with his herd. He looked at Abigail too long and too often, and she caught her father and Nabal exchanging glances several times throughout the meal. As soon as the poached apricots had been served, Abigail excused herself and escaped to the upper room where she slept.

Anna was waiting for her, directing Talia and Channah, two of her other maids, to prepare Abigail's bed for the night. Kai and Yelena were helping the cook in the kitchen. Her father had given her these four maidservants besides Anna, her nurse, and they had become more like friends than servants.

Anna helped her with her shawl, gathering the fine material and folding it neatly. "Who is the man your father invited to stay?"

"His name is Nabal. He is from the town of Maon. He raises sheep in the area of Carmel. Evidently he has a lot of sheep."

"So he is wealthy." Anna helped her slip off her embroidered dress and eased her into the looser, cooler dress she wore to sleep.

"I suppose." Abigail was not impressed by wealth. Ira was not wealthy, but he was kind, and that mattered more.

Anna did not respond, but her face showed that there was something she was not saying.

"What is it, Anna?"

"I wonder if there is a reason he is here tonight."

"He does business with my father. He was in the area and he needed a place to stay."

"Yes, that is true," Anna said softly. "But I wonder if there is another purpose to his staying here."

"A purpose? What do you mean?"

Anna made a great show of carefully folding the discarded dress. "You are a beautiful girl, of marriageable age...."

As her voice trailed off, Abigail felt a jolt in her chest. "You don't suppose he's here for..."

"To speak to your father, mistress?"

Could Anna be right? But surely her father wouldn't entertain the thought. It was Ira she wanted. Her mind raced. She must let her father know right away that she would only have Ira. She had no brothers or sisters, and her father had always indulged her. Surely he would listen to her.

Morning came quickly, and while Abigail had slept poorly, wrestling with her thoughts, she rose immediately. When her maids had seen her suitably dressed, she hurried down the stairs to speak with her father. She found him in the courtyard speaking with Nabal, who had his traveling cloak and his bag in hand.

Nabal smiled at her, but there seemed no warmth behind the smile. The eyes that gazed at her held something else. "I regret that I have to leave so early, but your father and I have completed our business and I must return to my home. We shall see each other again soon."

With a knowing look at her father, he strode out the door and was gone.

Abigail turned to her father. "Abba, I must speak with you. There is something I must tell you."

"Ah, my Abigail, first, there is news I have for you that cannot wait." There was a look of resignation on his face.

Abigail held her breath. She did not want to hear what her father was about to say.

"I have chosen a husband for you."

"But Abba—"

"Nabal is a good man and wealthy. He will take good care of you, and you shall be mistress of a large home. You will be able to take your maids with you."

"But I don't want—"

.